Children into pupils

Language, Education and Society

General Editor
Michael Stubbs
Department of Linguistics
University of Nottingham

Children into pupils
A study of language in early schooling

Mary J. Willes

West Midlands College of Higher Education

Routledge & Kegan Paul
London, Boston, Melbourne and Henley

*First published in 1983
by Routledge & Kegan Paul plc
39 Store Street, London WC1E 7DD,
9 Park Street, Boston, Mass. 02108, USA,
6th Floor, 464 St Kilda's Road,
Melbourne, Victoria 3004, Australia and
Broadway House, Newtown Road,
Henley-on-Thames, Oxon RG9 1EN
Set in IBM Press Roman by Columns, Reading
and printed in Great Britain by
T.J. Press Ltd, Padstow, Cornwall.*

Library of Congress Cataloging in Publication Data

Willes, Mary J.

*Children into pupils.
(Language, education, and society)
Bibliography: p.
Includes index.
1. Children — Language. 2. Language arts (Preschool)
I. Title. II. Series.*

| *LB1139.L3W484* | *1983* | *372.6* | *83-9675* |

ISBN 0-7100-9550-3 (U.S.)

Contents

General Editor's Preface

Simply a list of some of the questions implied by the phrase *Language, Education and Society* gives an immediate idea of the complexity, and also the fascination, of the area.

How is language related to learning? Or to intelligence? How should a teacher react to non-standard dialect in the classroom? Do regional and social accents and dialects matter? What is meant by standard English? Does it make sense to talk of 'declining standards' in language or in education? Or to talk of some children's language as 'restricted'? Do immigrant children require special language provision? How can their native languages be used as a valuable resource in schools? Can 'literacy' be equated with 'education'? Why are there so many adult illiterates in Britain and the USA? What effect has growing up with no easy access to language: for example, because a child is profoundly deaf? Why is there so much prejudice against people whose language background is odd in some way: because they are handicapped, or speak a non-standard dialect or foreign language? Why do linguistic differences lead to political violence, in Belgium, India, Wales and other parts of the world?

These are all real questions, of the kind which worry parents, teachers and policy-makers, and the answers to them are complex and not at all obvious. It is such questions that authors in this series will discuss.

Language plays a central part in education. This is probably generally agreed, but there is considerable debate and confusion about the exact relationship between language and learning. Even though the importance of language is generally recognised, we still have a lot to learn about how language is related to either educational success or to intelligence and thinking. Language is also a central fact in everyone's social life. People's attitudes and most deeply held beliefs are at stake, for it is through language that personal and social identities are maintained and recognised. People are judged, whether justly or not, by the language they speak.

Language, education and society is therefore an area where scholars have a responsibility to write clearly and persuasively, in order to communicate the best in recent research to as wide an audience as possible. This means not only other researchers, but also all those who are involved in educational, social and political policy-making, from individual teachers to government. It is an area where value judgments cannot be avoided. Any action that we take – or, of course, avoidance of action – has moral, social and political consequences. It is vital, therefore, that practice is informed by the best knowledge available, and that decisions affecting the futures of individual children or whole social groups are not taken merely on the basis of the all too wide-spread folk myths about language in society.

Linguistics, psychology and sociology are often rejected by non-specialists as jargon-ridden; or regarded as fascinating, but of no relevance to educational or social practice. But this is superficial and short-sighted: we are dealing with complex issues, which require an understanding of the general principles involved. It is bad theory to make statements about language in use which cannot be related to educational and social reality. But it is equally unsound to base beliefs and action on anecdote, received myths and unsystematic or idiosyncratic observations.

All knowledge is value-laden: it suggests action and changes our beliefs. Change is difficult and slow, but possible nevertheless. When language in education and society is seriously and systematically studied, it becomes clear how awesomely complex is the linguistic and social knowledge of all children and adults. And with such an understanding, it becomes impossible to maintain a position of linguistic prejudice and intolerance. This may be the most important implication of a serious study of language, in our linguistically diverse modern world.

This book by Mary Willes succeeds in combining linguistic theory and practical educational concerns to an extent which is seldom achieved. She presents a skilful selection and interpretation of linguistic work, in a way which makes it accessible and of immediate practical relevance to teachers. It is rare to find this integration, and this book provides a model for writings on language in education.

Willes has chosen a crucial research focus for her research: the very first days and weeks which children spend in school, when many assumptions about what is expected of school pupils are most visible.

No single method can capture the reality of classrooms, and Willes also skilfully combines different research methods. First, she reports fascinating ethnographic observations of infant classrooms. Second, she provides a detailed justification for more systematic linguistic description. Third, she uses experimental and interview methods to elicit further information from pupils.

These various methods and concepts are then put to practical exploratory use. The description of how young children acquire part of their communicative competence will be of interest to anyone concerned with children's linguistic and cognitive development: educational psychologists, sociolinguists, and others, who are primarily interested in the original descriptive findings. But the question of how easily (or not) young children learn what is expected of them in classrooms is of immediate practical concern to teachers, and to anyone who is concerned with helping children in the early stages of schooling, including teacher-trainers, speech therapists, and indeed parents.

Michael Stubbs
Nottingham

Acknowledgments

Anyone whose interest in language in educational settings leads to much time spent in classrooms incurs many debts. It is a pleasure to record my debt to Mr Keith Allison, who made possible many of the introductions, and to other educational administrators and head teachers whose assistance I sought and who were most helpful in their response. I am indebted too to the teachers who allowed me to record and observe in their classrooms, not only for tolerating my presence but for the lively and interesting discussions that often followed from the work. Since I have sought to preserve the anonymity of these people they cannot be mentioned by name.

There are other sorts of indebtedness that I gratefully acknowledge. I am grateful to Dr Malcolm Coulthard and to Professor John Sinclair and their colleagues in English Language Research at the University of Birmingham, notably to Miss Margaret Ashby, Dr David Brazil and Mr Ian Forsyth, for encouragement and support over an extended period of time.

I am indebted to colleagues and former colleagues, and especially to Dr Robin Fawcett and to Mr Euan Reid. My thanks are due to Mr Clem Adelman, Dr Michael Stubbs, Dr Gordon Wells and Dr James Wight, for opportunities to participate at different times in discussions and meetings. In addition I would like to thank both Mr and Mrs Andrew Selby for photographic assistance and Mrs Margaret Bowman and Mrs Margaret Donaldson for their care and patience at different stages of the typing.

My thanks are also due to the following editors and publishers for permission to include material previously published by them: C. Adelman (editor), *Uttering, Muttering – collecting, using and reporting talk for social and educational research*, London, Grant McIntyre, 1981; P. French and M. Maclure (editors), *Adult-Child Conversation*, London, Croom Helm, 1981; The Open University, Supplementary Readings for Block 5 of Course PE 232, Language Development, 1979.

Introduction:
the purposes of the study

Books about children's language designed for teachers are by now numerous and the production of another may be thought to require some explanation. This one owes much to the students with whom I have worked during the years it was in preparation. It is my hope that it will be found useful by their successors, and that it may in addition interest experienced teachers, particularly those engaged in one of the various forms of in-service professional education now available, and those concerned with teacher education. It is a book about talk, talk as the joint production of teachers and pupils. It takes for granted a good deal that, in a book designed to assist relatively inexperienced teachers in practical ways, it would be necessary to argue. It assumes, for example, a recognition that language, spoken and written, is central to the processes of education and that we are all in some sense indebted to the Bullock Report (1975) for authoritatively asserting that this is so, and for elaborating this conviction in some detail. This book assumes too that any notion that language is important only or chiefly because it is the means by which knowledge is transmitted between the generations is pretty well discredited. Talking in class, for so long the commonest of all juvenile misdemeanours, is recognised now as an indispensable means by which learning takes place. I am not of course suggesting that all the chatter in which children engage is educationally productive, nor that making opportunities and occasions for educationally useful talk is easy. On the contrary, to do it successfully requires a degree of attentiveness and discrimination and sensitivity much harder to attain than is the authority required to impose attentive silence on a class. Talking to learn is very far from being an easy option. There is a literature in which ways of doing it are explored and discussed and in which examples of good practice are examined in helpful detail (Barnes, Britton and Rosen, 1971; Barnes and Todd, 1981; Tough, 1973; Rosen and Rosen, 1973). This book is sympathetic to the approach taken by these authors. My own approach and purposes are, however, rather different. The basis of that approach and those purposes is a conviction of long standing that has survived changes of fortune and fashion. It is this: that however variously and imaginatively teachers make use of what used to be called (collectively) 'visual aids' in their teaching, language is for all of them the major means of communication; the primary, essential, indispensable mode of professional functioning. They need to know about it; as they gain experience in deploying it effectively, they need to reflect on what it is they do. In some sense of course they *do* know about it, and they always have. The experience of educated, literate adults includes a very great deal of knowledge about operating at least one language — often more than one. Most of them are able to do so capably, variously and appropriately; some do it with wit and style. In addition every teacher shares with other adults in the community a complex of opinions and beliefs and values relating to language. Not all of these stand up to critical scrutiny. My belief is that developments in linguistics and its applications in the most recent half-century have made significantly more than this attainable by teachers, and that it should be made accessible to them. Such knowledge is not simply more detailed or more up to date; it is qualitatively different from that which is absorbed as part of the process of growing up in an advanced society, with long traditions of learning and literacy. Knowledge attained by deliberate study, subjected to discussion, tested and modified in application, is available for critical scrutiny. It is changed, or discarded, in the light of fresh evidence, or fresh interpretation of old evidence. It can be used in making decisions and in evaluating them. This constitutes, to my mind, the case for teachers undertaking a study of classroom language that is linguistics-based and linguistically defensible. It is the justification for my decision, in writing this book, to give much space in the first two chapters to linguistic studies of the processes by which language is acquired by children and the processes of conversation are understood by them. It determines, too, the themes of the book, and in the interests of clarity I should say here what these are. This is a book about a second stage of the process of acquiring language and learning simultaneously to participate in discourse, that stage for which, in our own country and others in which the upbringing of children is similarly institutionalised, the classroom is the setting, and learning goes on in interaction with a teacher and with other children of the same age. It is about a part of the development of what is termed, in the literature to which I shall refer in the opening chapters, communicative competence, and a part in which teachers play a crucial role. The stance taken is that conversational exchange, including the sort of talk that goes on between teachers and children, normally seems to participants to be spontaneous, random, and unpredictable, and is in fact none of these things. People engaged in talk are as unaware of the rule-governed nature of the activity as they are of the rules of the sound system and grammatical system of the language they speak. The professional work of linguists includes observing the regularities that occur and articulating them, identifying and formulating the systematic nature of the process. I am especially indebted to work done in this area by a team led by Professor J. McH. Sinclair and Dr R.M. Coulthard, and I shall later make detailed and frequent references to their work. For the teacher who has access to such studies, who recognises that newcomers to school are in the process of finding out what the rules of classroom talk are, who knows (as of course pupils do not) what these rules are in some degree of detail, there are, I believe, possibilities of valuable insight. This, broadly, is the position I shall want to examine in what follows.

My concern is with English language in English classrooms, and my experience and observation have been in urban classrooms. I could not avoid, therefore, even if I wished to, a subsidiary topic. For a minority of children in the population at large, but a majority in some schools, and in the experience of some teachers, this significant early development is complicated by the fact that it coincides with the need to learn a new language. These are children from homes in which English is the language of broadcast sound, but almost never of talk addressed to the child or in which he takes part. Starting school must seem to these children an unusually stressful experience in which apparently well-intentioned adults neither understand what they say nor speak intelligibly to them. Nobody claims that this state of affairs is anything but the unintended effect of economic pressures and population shifts. What actually happens in schools where monolingual teachers have to accept responsibility for children in the earliest stages of becoming bilingual, what options are actually available within the constraints that operate, and what are the observable effects of operating these choices, seem then to be topics of some importance, deserving examination within a sociolinguistic frame of reference.

The design of the book

The first two chapters have a historical emphasis. I have tried to indicate some of the principal ways in which, in the recent past, fundamental, universally interesting questions about how children learn to talk and to understand have been asked, and to outline some major changes of motivation and shifts of emphasis. Without some recognition of the rapidity with which, in an area of expanding interest, changes of focus occur, I do not think it possible for the individual teacher, wishing to reflect on, examine, and criticise his own involvement in language use, to recognise his own historically determined perspectives, or know what range of questions he can ask — nor, of course, can he identify what, of a dauntingly extensive and varied literature, he can usefully read. This was my experience, coming initially to this study, and it has been that of many students I have taught and from whom I have learnt. I shall argue that the subject seems initially formidable because an interdisciplinary perspective is a necessity, so the number of relevant studies is large, though the number directly antecedent, or specifically concerned with the processes of becoming a fully participating pupil, is very much smaller. The next chapter, the third, is addressed to the subject of the multilingual classroom. This chapter is based on observations of situations where children bring a variety of mother tongues to the early stages of an education exclusively through the medium of English. That observation, on which I rely both here and later, is subject, of course, to all the limitations and shortcomings that inevitably attend it. It allows only the most cautious and guarded of generalisations to be made (unless, of course, it is strongly supported from other sources); it is in some degree arbitrary and accidental; the presence of the observer affects what occurs in ways it is simply not possible to specify. Its justification has to be that it is simply indispensable. Some significant features of the situation are not represented at all by alternative means of examination.

The central section of the book is concerned with some of the varying kinds of conversational interaction that the organisation of the day, in the early stages of schooling, allows for. This is where I have tried to examine in some detail the orderly and rule-governed character of classroom language, to examine with reference to recorded and transcribed texts some of the ways in which meanings are negotiated between teachers and young pupils, with varying degrees of success.

In the lengthy chapter that follows (Chapter 7) I describe an attempt to get beyond the limits of observation by developing a means of eliciting from young children what are their perceptions of their situation, and of their own part in it. In the final chapter some concluding observations are offered, and there is some attempt to compare and evaluate the various metaphors of interaction processes that are most commonly used in attempts to discuss and understand and explain them.

1

The language children bring to school

There is a historical bias to this chapter and the next. That is not to claim that the two, taken together, constitute a literature survey, if that term is taken as a claim to exhaustiveness, or even to some degree of completeness. Rather I offer a sketch map, of limited but, I hope, positive use. Interest in the process by which a baby —

> 'An infant crying for the light,
> And with no language but a cry'

— becomes a talking, comprehending child is widely shared and is of so long standing that it is not possible to put a date on it. It is however possible to claim that in the recent past, and most notably in the last twenty-five years, that interest has been pursued with a degree of vigour and tenacity and seriousness that does not seem to have a precedent. The study of language acquisition has in that time come to occupy a central position in the concerns of linguists. It has for longer than that time been a matter of compelling interest for people involved in children's education, for parents and therapists and administrators as well as for teachers. Anyone who shares that interest inherits a recent history that has been eventful, charged with vitality, full of change. Questions that not long ago in terms of chronological time seemed critically important now seem less so. What it once seemed safe and necessary to ignore now claims attention. Topics that for a time generated much activity in speculation and research have been set aside as exhausted, and then rediscovered and reinterpreted. The result of so much activity is a very large literature, much of it written for a specialist public already thoroughly familiar with the writers' assumptions and terms of reference, and consequently not at all readily accessible to the reader who comes fresh to it, several years later. Book lists on the acquisition and development of language, even where these are carefully prepared, classified under headings and annotated for the use of interested enquirers, seem to them forbidding, simply by their length. If so huge an investment of time is required just to read one's way into the subject, is their (usually unspoken) response, what will survive of that responsiveness to children engaged in the language-acquiring process that prompted the initial enquiry? At the same time the literature cannot be ignored. Students I have worked with feel insecure in the absence of information about the history of a topic which, whether from choice or because of the requirements of a chosen course, they have undertaken to study. Without some indication of at least the salient features, the time scale, the major contributors, and the recent and current items of debate, what they are asked to read seems to them full of contradictions, preoccupied by controversies the meaning and significance of which are alike unclear, an assembly of large generalisations and unmemorable data that they can neither interpret nor apply. That insecurity is resolved, at least to a degree that makes continuation possible, when they know enough of what has happened in the recent past to see themselves as inheritors of traditions, participants who enter at a particular stage of the debate (and need to inform themselves, so to speak, by access to the minutes), enquirers, whose interests are in great part determined, as are the means of enquiry available to them, by their point of entry to the ongoing, developing discussion. They are in a position then to admire innovatory and influential ideas even if they are no longer current. The records of past controversies no longer confuse and irritate, and there are better reasons than the limits on energy and time for making selections from the literature available.

Where the study of language acquisition and development is concerned, the past twenty-five years have (from the standpoint of the early 1980s) a distinct identity. The period starts with a readily recognisable, prominent landmark in the publication of Chomsky's critique of Skinner's *Verbal Behaviour*, and with it, of the broadly behaviourist interpretation of the language learning process that seemed at that time susceptible of development, certainly, but safe from serious and fundamental challenge. The effect of that challenge was to move the study from the edges of the concerns of theoretical linguists into the centre, and to open up a new range of questions about the processes by which children learn to talk. What if the learning process were indeed different in kind from the sort of learning that takes place in institutional settings? How is it that learning the mother tongue is something that all normal children, including those who learn what is taught in schools slowly, painfully, and with notable lack of success, accomplish easily?

These and related questions were suggested, and with them a whole new direction of research, having as its major focus those elements of the process that are common to all children and have close counterparts in widely differing languages. Such a concentration of focus entailed the virtual exclusion of much else that had then to be rediscovered – the more slowly because of the immense authority and prestige of Chomsky himself, and the notable success and interest of the work that took its impetus from the theoretical position he developed. How its inherent limitations became apparent, and interest shifted and widened to include, in addition to the processes by which children learn the sound and grammatical systems of the mother tongue, those by which they learn to mean and to comprehend meaning, and those by which they become participants in situated language use, will be indicated in this initial chapter. The effect of this history has been to make language acquisition studies more widely and variously interesting, without in any way diminishing the academic vigour with which they have been pursued. The interests of linguists and of educationists are not identical, nor should they be, but recent developments, particularly developments in sociolinguistics, have brought them closer together, have increased the possibility for and the reality of fruitful exchange, and have made possible for linguists the appreciation of traditions of work in the study of language, literacy and classroom language for which educationists and sociologists of education have been responsible. For reasons broadly similar to those I have already outlined I have given the second chapter of the book to some account of these. In the process of sketching in a little more detail the historical development I have indicated I shall try to show how the concerns of this book, which are widely shared, relate to our changing understanding of the relations between the individual child, the language he learns, and the society and its institutions to which he is a newcomer.

A challenge to accepted ideas about the acquisition of language

Two publications, that of B.F. Skinner's *Verbal Behaviour* (1957) and Chomsky's review of the book in *Language* vol. 35, 1959, comprise not so much a landmark, as a natural feature that dominates the landscape of recent history from a great distance. In the opening paragraphs of the review, Chomsky recognises the significance of the book, as the most substantial and authoritative statement at that time available of a position then widely regarded as beyond serious challenge. The acquisition of language is presented, as the title of Skinner's book suggests, as a special, and highly interesting, variant of distinctively human behaviour. Learning to talk, runs the argument, is accomplished in fundamentally the same way as other sorts of learning. Much that can be shown to be true of the way in which other animals learn contributes to our understanding of the process. Stimuli are presented, responses are made, and are reinforced; this pattern is repeated with indefinitely many variants, some of them very subtle. For the developing child, the language environment provides innumerable stimuli, and his responses to them are reinforced by parental interest and approval. That reinforcement, initially not at all discriminating, becomes increasingly selective, so that as the child gets older, a closer and more accurate approximation to adult norms is required in order to secure the reinforcement he looks for. Having recognised the cogency of the presentation, Chomsky takes the opportunity of the review to issue a challenge to this, the behaviourist view, as an explanation of the essential, central, character of language acquisition. He does not deny that children frequently imitate what they hear, nor that parental approval has a role to play in the learning process. His claim is that these are quite marginal matters, since they offer no plausible explanation of the essential character of the process — that it is innovative and creative. From the start, children use their limited language to say new and, as a rule, appropriate things, things they have not heard, and very often things that no adult would say in any circumstances. What children actually hear from the adults about them is, Chomsky claims, more often than not fragmentary, and at best incomplete, since informal spoken language is highly elliptical. In Chomsky's terms, the language available to the child who is learning his mother tongue is, considered as data, 'degenerate'. Conversely, what children produce is systematic at every stage. Further, Chomsky insists that the astonishing process is accomplished very rapidly by all normal children. Between the second and the fifth years of life, they learn nearly all the phonological and syntactic rules of their mother tongue, and become intelligible, almost all the time, to other users of it. Not only clever children manage this extraordinary feat; those who learn what schools a little later try to teach them only slowly, manage *this* learning successfully, without much deliberate effort, and without noticeable stress. Only those children faced with an exceptional degree of handicap, a gross defect of intelligence, or a severe impairment of hearing, fail to acquire their mother tongue within the normal, limited, time span. A radically different explanation from that offered by the behaviourist psychology

that has in Skinner such an able and persuasive exponent has to be
found, and that which Chomsky put forward in the concluding pages of
his review, and developed in subsequent writings (notably in Chomsky,
1965) posits a process quite different from that by which school studies
(including the learning in educational settings of foreign languages) are
mastered. It is often referred to as the *innatist hypothesis*. In its 'strong'
form, that is, in its least compromising and most emphatic version, it
explains the ease and rapidity with which the mother tongue is normally
acquired in these terms: the fundamental rules of human language,
those that are true of all languages, and that linguists refer to as 'language universals', do not have to be learnt. They are part of each child's
genetically transmitted inheritance. We are born to speak, in the same
sense as we are born to walk upright — though we do neither for some
months after birth. What is needed in order to set in motion the process
of discovering what are the distinctive realisations of those universal
rules at the time and in the place where each individual finds himself, is
the experience of hearing language spoken. A child will (irrespective of
the nationality or the language of his parents) learn Arabic or English,
Japanese or Russian, depending solely on the language of his environment. The experience of hearing the language functions like a switch
that turns on an elaborate mechanism. A child born with a severe
degree of hearing loss fails to acquire his mother tongue, not because he
lacks any part of that inherited knowledge of the universal rules, but
because he is like a mechanism with a faulty or a missing switch — time
is lost before the fault is discovered, and elaborate, costly, and not very
satisfactory alternative ways have then to be found of setting the
mechanism going. Normal children, those who are receptive to the
experience of hearing language, treat what they hear as data from
which they infer the rest of the system, and they test their inferences
in use, in a manner comparable to that in which an adult linguist,
sensitised by his education to anticipate and actively to search for
regularities, infers the sound and grammatical systems of a language
that he does not know, and tests out his suppositions and checks or
corrects them in interaction with native speakers. It is not, of course,
suggested that children proceed with their search for the rules of their
mother tongue in a conscious way, or could comprehend an explanation of what they do couched in these terms. The knowledge of the
mother tongue that is acquired is, and for most people remains, operational knowledge. Children cannot make what it is that they do, articulate, and the overwhelming majority of adult speakers have no need
to do so. Neither the knowledge that is implied by speaking, nor the

process of acquiring that knowledge, is available to introspection. Whatever it is that makes that knowledge possible requires a label; the genetic endowment that Chomsky posits is, in a sense, a 'black box', something not directly observable, though the data that go into it and the system that comes out of it can be readily observed. 'Language acquisition device' (often abbreviated to LAD) is the label on the box. The position put forward by Chomsky in 1959, and afterwards elaborated, profoundly influenced the character and the direction of the study of children's acquisition of their mother tongue for more than a decade. If one characteristic of a valuable hypothesis is its capacity for stimulating the imagination and enthusiasm of gifted investigators, and so of generating research, then this one must rank very high. Among linguists, the study of language acquisition shifted into a position of central theoretical importance. If we knew, in substantial detail, just what it is that children do, then we should know what exactly are the profound similarities between and among languages, underlying their baffling diversity. To discover what syntactic rules children learn, in what sequence, and by what changes these rules approximate to those operated by adults, in short, to write the grammars children infer, and operate, and discard, presented a fascinating and difficult intellectual challenge. While this activity was at its height, the solid merits of Skinner's book, its sustained vitality, its clarity, its abundance of interesting illustrative exemplification, its cogent presentation of the continuity of the language acquisition process into the years of schooling and beyond, went largely unregarded.

Not everyone shared Chomsky's own conviction that the interest of the position he put forward was entirely theoretical, and that no application to educational concerns was apparent or foreseeable. Kellogg Hunt drew teachers' attention to Chomsky's early (1957) model of grammar as one that explained what is readily observed — that as children develop skills in written composition they learn to control initially simple sentences, comprising a single clause; they then learn to combine these, using what have traditionally been termed co-ordinating conjunctions, and later they master the subordinating conjunctions. This order of acquisition is typical, if not invariable. The assumption that the study of a model of grammar would accelerate the process of learning to write acceptably (long discredited in relation to traditional grammar) enjoyed, in some United States schools, a brief revival, and simplified expositions of Transformational Generative Grammar were prepared for the use of teachers and classes. Bateman and Zidonis (1966) carried out a careful piece of empirical research designed to test the effect (or the absence of an effect) of such study upon the developing composition skills of secondary pupils, and found that their experimental groups produced more well-formed sentences and made fewer errors than the control groups, but that in terms of the structural complexity of the sentences they produced, there was no significant difference between the two. In general, however, those who were centrally concerned with developing and testing hypotheses relating to the acquisition of language concentrated their efforts on the earliest stages of the process, and disregarded possible educational applications. Contemporary studies of classroom language by educationists pursued other routes. Studies of language acquisition, energetically pursued in the 1960s, (and authoritatively reviewed and discussed, Brown, 1974) seemed initially to provide strong support for the view that the processes by which children acquire the syntactic rules of English demonstrate a broadly similar pattern. The data obtained by groups of researchers who shared a single theoretical framework, but who were geographically widely separated, admitted of impressively similar interpretation.

Children at the stage of producing two-word utterances seemed to have access to two distinct classes of words, one larger than the other and including words newly added to the vocabulary. Neither class conformed to those familiar to adult-speakers — nouns, verbs, and so on. Different groups of workers assigned different labels to these classes, among which *pivot* and *open* class speedily gained acceptance in general use. Further, each group of researchers concluded that these young children did not combine the elements in a random way. Certain sorts of combination did not occur. They were ungrammatical — and the rule that excluded them had no counterpart in the language the child heard and would eventually speak. This seemed to offer powerful support from empirical evidence for Chomsky's theoretical position, evidence of language behaviour that was rule-governed and systematic in a way that could not have been learned by imitation. Immense effort went into the time-consuming study of the grammatical systems individual children acquired and then discarded. While English could claim in this area (as in a number of others) to be the most studied language, the process of acquiring other languages, including those very different from English in terms of their structure, was seen as a very important activity. It was human language, not particular languages, that was the focus of theoretical interest. In the work of Eric Lenneberg there were clear implications for at least some classrooms. His professional work as a pediatrician brought him in touch with children for whom the normal processes of language acquisition were either delayed, as a result of physical or intellectual handicap, or were distorted by some illness or accident resulting in brain injury. His study of a group of children born with Down's syndrome ('mongolism') led him to conclude that in those suffering from a mild to moderate degree of mental retardation, the processes by which language is acquired, and the order in which the rules are learned, are indistinguishable from the experience of normal populations. It is the *rate* at which the successive rules are mastered that is critically different. The timetable of language acquisition for these cognitively impaired children extended over the whole of childhood to the start of puberty. Only then does it stop. His studies of brain-injured children supported the suggestion of a physiological and neurological explanation for the contrast between the ease and speed of normal mother tongue learning and the high failure rate associated with the learning, in institutional settings, of subsequent languages. Among his patients were some children whose normal language was, apparently, destroyed by illness or accident. If the accident occurred before puberty, the prognosis was good; they began again and went through the stages in a matter of months. In adolescents and in adults, recovery was altogether slower and more uncertain. It seemed to Lenneberg that there was a 'critical period' for language learning that began towards the end of the first year of life and was completed with the development of dominance in hand and brain. If this is the case, there is no need to look further for an explanation of the reason why modern foreign languages are so poorly learned by the majority of secondary school pupils. It does of course leave unexplained, and apparently inexplicable, the success of a minority of adolescents and adult learners. Again, if Lenneberg is right, the case for ensuring for the retarded a continuation of the sort of environment in which young normal children learn to speak, is very strong indeed.

His finding that the rate at which language is acquired differs substantially between individual children runs counter to the emphasis Chomsky puts upon the overall rapidity of the process. It has strong support from the interim conclusions of the much more recent research directed by Gordon Wells, to which more detailed reference is made below. The sample of children whose utterances provided the data base for the work of this research team was constructed so as to exclude any handicap that might reasonably be expected to impede the process of normal language acquisition; none the less the team found broad similarities in the order of learning and marked contrasts in the rate of learning. My own observations of children in process of learning to interact with their teachers point to a broadly similar conclusion. Few teachers would find such conclusions in any way surprising. It should be a matter for concern that in general education is organised on a contrary principle; it begins formally for 5-year-olds and rising 5s; it ends at 16. Organisation is normally on a basis of year groups; 'setting' and 'streaming', initially designed to take account of the disparities among children of similar chronological age, are widely criticised for their divisive and discouraging effects, but in their absence we have at present no educational strategy for varying rates of progress.

Communicative competence: shifts of emphasis and interpretation

With the end of the 1960s came a shift of emphasis, and a recognition that becoming a member of a speech community entails more than operational knowledge of the rules of the sound and grammatical systems. Lois Bloom's (1970) study illustrates the direction of change particularly well, since she began with the intention of categorising her data (the recorded utterances of her own young daughter) in terms of 'pivot' and 'open' classes. She found that in the act of assigning utterances to these categories, she had no alternative to taking into account the context in which they were uttered. She had in fact to do, as linguist and researcher, what parents and teachers do all the time – to make her own best guess at the meaning intended by the child. This was not in itself difficult; hers was one of many detailed studies of the writer's own child, to whom she had, of course, virtually unlimited access. The issue was a theoretical, not a practical one. In order to make decisions about grammatical structures, she had first to determine upon meanings, and to classify, as these emerged, the functions that her daughter controlled, the things she was learning to *do* with language. The immediate result of this enquiry was not as radical as this suggests; it was a reinterpretation of the terms 'pivot' and 'open' as labels for categories of children's utterances and a reinterpretation of the term 'telegraphic speech', which had been in use to capture the elliptical character of young children's utterances. Bloom posited more complicated underlying structures, too cumbersome for utterance at that early stage, and needing to be reduced so as to be manageable. None the less, the impracticability of ignoring children's meanings and adults' interpretation of their meanings had been convincingly demonstrated.

Pressure towards a shift in the focus of interest came from more than one quarter. It was not just that the child's developing internalised knowledge of the rule system, his 'competence' as opposed to his observable 'performance', was, and would remain, inaccessible to introspection and to direct observation, and had to be inferred from what was actually said, from each child's *performance*. Performance was not just more limited than his competence, but was subject to all sorts of accidental disturbances and distractions. This is Chomsky's (1965) account of the distinction between these two:

> Linguistic theory is concerned primarily with the ideal speaker/
> listener, in a completely homogeneous speech community, who
> knows its language perfectly, and is unaffected by such
> grammatically irrelevant conditions as memory limitations,
> distractions, shifts of attention and interest and errors (random or
> characteristic) in applying his knowledge to actual performance.
> (p. 3)

The degree to which 'competence' in Chomsky's sense should be taken to include a knowledge of what may appropriately and properly be said in particular circumstances and what might be better termed 'sociolinguistic' or 'communicative' competence was, by the end of the 1960s, a topic of discussion (Huxley and Ingram, 1971), and Hasan, in a 1971 paper, pointed out that if the ease and speed with which children learn the syntactic rules of their mother tongue is acknowledged to be remarkable, so too is the readiness with which they learn what may suitably and sensibly be said in particular circumstances. A vigorous and persuasive case for retaining the *term* competence, but for modifying its meaning, was made by Campbell and Wales (1970). In a paper designed as a summary of the stage language acquisition studies had reached at the time of writing, they directed their readers' attention back to a period before the preceding decade, before Chomsky's influence was established, when any study of children learning to talk took it for granted that the basic unit of enquiry was the communicative act, what the speaker meant in the place and at the time when he spoke. They asserted that while Chomsky's immense authority and prestige had given a renewed impetus to the study of language acquisition, a price, and a high one, had been paid. The effect of his influence had been to focus attention on the acquisition of syntactically structured speech, to the virtual exclusion of everything else. Their disappointing conclusion was that an immense amount of time and effort, and huge intellectual and financial resources, had been expended upon the study of the process of learning to talk, without anything like a commensurate increase in our actual understanding of it. They argued that the under-standing of developing competence at which this effort was directed was one

> from which by far the most important linguistic ability has been omitted – the ability to produce or understand utterances which are not so much grammatical but, more important, appropriate to the context in which they are made. (p. 247)

This is the crux of their paper. What it implies, and how much it entails, has become at least partially apparent in the changed direction of recent studies, about which the authors of this paper demonstrated a remarkable degree of foresight. Language acquisition studies in the 1970s have been more varied, broader and more inclusive in their scope, and their overriding concern has been with the development of the ability to mean, and to comprehend meaning. There have been studies of the development of language structures certainly, but with structures as the means of realisation of the varied functions language has. As a direct result, work has been done on children younger and older than those that were, in the 1960s, the subjects of more narrowly focused enquiry, studies of the varied environments in which the process of language acquisition occurs, and of children as participants in inter-action. The major landmark in this broadening landscape is not a single publication, but a series of papers in which, between 1966 and 1972, Dell Hymes developed and elaborated the concept of *communicative competence*. He seems not to have been alone in using it but he urged the case for its acceptance, examined its implications, and argued authoritatively that the idea it captures is indispensable to the discus-sion of language acquisition and of situated discourse more generally, necessary alike to those who are committed to the development of coherent explanatory theories about language, and to those whose interests are in the application of theory to matters of practical con-cern, educational and other. There has been some tendency to assume that the second group can afford an eclecticism, even a degree of super-ficiality, that theorists would not tolerate. Hymes set the weight of his authority firmly against any such double standard. By his use of the term *competence* he asserts the historical continuity between the study of situated language use and the studies of the 1960s, having their principled basis in the theoretical work of Chomsky. He argues that on theoretical as well as on practical grounds, the concept of competence associated with that work has to be modified. Without modification, concepts having undisputed theoretical status, ('speaker/listener', 'speech act', 'acceptability', 'speech community') are no more than labels for socio-cultural variables. Further, without modification, the notion of competence is just not possible to apply, because it excludes from consideration the very difficulties in language use that urgently require remedial intervention by teachers and others. Hymes sees the work of Chomsky as the culmination of a classic structuralism. That work accounts for the internal structure of language and for its intrinsic human significance, and these (in his view) are notable advances. There are, however, other demands that may be legitimately made of linguistic theory and they are not met. No principled basis is provided, for example, for some of the things children do (or, contrary to expectation, fail to do) that patently require linguistic explanation. The fact that the utterances they produce are not only new and systematic, but are (typically) in some recognisable degree appropriate, is one of these. That very young children internalise attitudes towards language is another. How communicative competence is acquired and developed became, in the 1970s, a focus of enquiry no less vigorous than that of the preceding decade, and much more varied in approach. A whole range of new questions needed to be asked. How was it, for example, that children find out that between the form of an utterance and the intention of the speaker there may be no more than a partial correspondence, and sometimes an outright contradiction. Yet the second, the function, has to be retrieved from the first, the form. What is termed the *illocutionary force* of the utterance, what the speaker intends to *do* is often at variance with the grammatical structure. Adult language users have access to information about the situation and about the speaker, and knowledge of the ways in which implications are expressed in English, that assist them to retrieve obliquely expressed meanings. (Even then, success is less than constant or uniform.)

In a discussion of children's learning of the discourse rules, Sinclair and Coulthard (1975) draw attention to the extent to which this ability to interpret is taken for granted by adult native speakers, though they do not, at this point, pursue the matter further:

A native speaker who interpreted 'Is that the mint sauce over there?' or 'Can you tell me the time?' as yes/no questions, 'Have a drink' as a command, or 'I wish you'd go away' as requiring just a murmur of agreement, would find the world a bewildering place, full of irritable people. (p. 28)

Those who are engaged in learning English as a new language are expected to make just such mistakes, though they do not always escape an irritated response. Children in the early stages of learning English as a mother tongue make them too, but Reeder (1980) found evidence that at three years of age they can often recover the intentions of speakers from utterances where grammatical form is at variance with the speaker's intention.

Such mistakes are common in classrooms. Teachers are amused rather than annoyed when such questions as 'Would you like to tell me about your painting (or collage, or model)?', regularly posed, are interpreted as yes/no questions and answered by a firm and polite 'no thank you'. That such mistakes are occasional, rather than usual, is evidence that at 5 or 6 children can as a rule interpret this question as an instruction, a *directive*, made in a deliberately unthreatening manner by someone who has a right to give instructions, and their answers, irrespective of whether they satisfy the teacher, imply this sort of understanding. Much of the later work of Susan Ervin-Tripp has been addressed to these and related questions, and the volume of her collected papers (edited, with a detailed bibliography, by Anwar S. Dil) constitutes a close examination of the processes by which children acquire what adult speakers possess: access to alternative ways of saying the same thing, control of more than one variety of speech style, and the possibility of a range of communicative choice. Ervin-Tripp argues that within the sort of speech community with which we are most familiar, a large and complex one, a variety of sociolinguistic rule systems obtains at any one time, and the effect of this must be to extend and complicate and prolong the task of the learner beyond the first few years of life, and outside the family setting. Further, she argues (and by doing so takes the discussion into an area immediately relevant to educational concerns) the learner cannot always rely upon an encouraging, or even a tolerant, learning environment. For many children, beginning school imposes pressure to master a sociolinguistic rule system quite different from any they have encountered before. The difficulty of the task, and the unfavourable environment – at best uncomprehending, at worst actively hostile – in which it has to be undertaken, may very well, in her view, exacerbate ethnic differences in American English-speaking society, and contribute to the learning difficulties experienced by very many black working-class pupils. This is a view elaborated by Kochman (1972), and most interestingly extended in respect of Amerindian pupils, whose performance in English-medium schools is often a source of frustration and disappointment to their teachers, by Philips (1972). All these difficulties must be present in an acute form for children obliged to begin their schooling in a language that is not their mother tongue, and in the case of a teacher to whom that mother tongue is unknown. This is exactly the situation of some children in inner-city schools in this country.

Studies of the environment of language acquisition

The reappraisal of the language that adults use when addressing young children represents a related and, in contrast with 1960s work, a radical shift of emphasis. That such talk was, in Chomsky's use of the term, 'degenerate' was an article of faith among a whole generation of linguists. Brown (1974) points this out, and goes on to dissociate himself from it, quoting with approval Labov's vigorous attack upon this orthodoxy, on the grounds that adult speech to children is neither random nor incomplete. The dissimilarity between adults' talk to young children and their talk to each other was assumed in the 1960s to be fundamentally unhelpful to the child, and so to constitute a powerful argument for the reality and the significance of the LAD. Since the environment was typically unfavourable to learning, the genetically transmitted predisposition to do so must be correspondingly strong. That adults in our own culture, and in many others, *do* address children in the early stages of language acquisition in ways different from those they employ in talk with other listeners, is not in dispute. Those differences are systematic and can be described. It is not just that adults typically use a special 'nursery' vocabulary. In addition, they avoid complicated grammatical constructions. Their talk is extremely repetitive, with much redundancy. They exaggerate the normal intonation contours. They are concerned almost exclusively with the immediate environment, the here and now of shared experience. In the 1970s the character, and the function, of such talk became the subject of scrutiny. It was argued (Snow, 1972; Vorster, 1975) that the characteristic ways in which mothers talk to their small children, far from impeding or confusing language acquisition, might reasonably be supposed to facilitate it. Because it relates so closely to the context of shared experience, the non-linguistic clues to linguistic meaning are frequent, accessible, and repeated. The exaggerated intonation contours provide clear indication of what must be listened for. Repetition and redundancy reassure the learner, and offer opportunities for him to participate. Far from producing 'degenerate' language in addressing their children, mothers typically and spontaneously, it was claimed, produce a variety singularly well adapted to a young learner's requirements. If this is once accepted, then there is much less that requires to be explained by reference to a language acquisition device. It becomes necessary to suppose, as part of a child's genetic inheritance, no more than a very general predisposition to interpret experience in definable ways. The view that baby talk constitutes a nearly ideal medium for early language learning has been challenged. Papers assembled by Snow and Ferguson (1977) illustrate some of the directions that challenge has assumed. Interest in the interaction between the young child and those who take care of him has proved very durable, and its character has been the subject of a large number of studies comprehensively reviewed by Snow in her introduction to this collection, some of them notably subtle and delicate in observation and interpretation. Typically, they put forward bold hypotheses about what is actually happening in the interaction they discuss. In concluding her survey, Snow is more cautious than in her earlier papers about the function of adult language in the child's learning process. It is, in her view, quite plausible that baby talk may serve to minimise confusion and to consolidate gains, but, she suggests, if we are to gain understanding of really significant steps forward, to find out how children gain insight into how a particular structure goes, or how a rule applies, it may be necessary to stop assembling large samples of mothers' speech to children and to focus intently upon quite limited and specific passages of interaction.

Recent studies demonstrate a similar caution, and a similar concentration upon specific problems. Cross (1978) concentrated upon what is a matter of ordinary observation but had received rather little attention in earlier studies, that children acquire their mother tongue at different rates, and asked what features in the speech of mothers to their children seemed to facilitate learning? The results of his study supported Cazden's much earlier (1966) conclusion that children are best assisted by adults who deliberately help them, expanding and extending their partial and halting utterances. Some of the mothers in his sample regularly produced simpler and grammatically better formed utterances than others. It would be natural enough to suppose that these characteristics would speed the learning of their children, but Cross could find no evidence that this was so. He concludes, again cautiously, that what are the helpful features at one stage of development may be less helpful at another. We may need to map the changing needs of the child in relation to acquiring his mother tongue.

Kaye and Charney (1981) pick up an aspect of the process that has again attracted rather little attention, the learning by children of the alternating nature of discourse. Keenan (1974) found evidence that this is something that is learned very early. The young boys in her study took turns in utterance at a very early stage. Kaye and Charney emphasise the asymmetry of the process, the inequality of the interaction. From the start of speech, it is the adult who assumes the initiating role. She, usually the mother, creates and maintains the semblance of dialogue, interpreting any utterance, any movement, any sound (or even the absence of any of these) on the child's part as his 'turn' to which the adult can then respond: they observe that 'treating the child *as if* he were participating in intelligent conversation is a basic activity in mother/infant caretaking and play.' It is not, they add, a strategy for language teaching. Rather it creates an environment in which conversational and linguistic skill are learned, and they conclude:

> the child is presented with ongoing discourse in which he finds himself already a participant on topics very largely selected by his own interests. His meanings are interpreted, expressed, and expatiated upon before he even knows what meaning is. . . .

Something very like this, I shall argue at a later stage, seems to account for the ease with which 5-year-olds learn to take part in classroom discourse. It is natural that studies of adult/child interaction should concentrate on the mother, since she is the most important person in the young child's world. She is not, however, the only one, and studies of the language environment available to the language acquirer have widened to include other members of the family (Corsaro, 1979; Rondal, 1980), older children and adults, including teachers, who are part of the child's expanding world (French and Maclure, 1981). Language acquisition studies in the 1970s have been characterised by breadth, detail, and variety, and the debate has proceeded on the basis of an underlying agreement, given expression by Wells (1975), that it is a mistake to concentrate exclusively upon internal, autonomous, individual development. Studies of the relation between the process and the environment of situated interaction in which it occurs constitute one way of avoiding that mistake. Another is the reconsideration of the relation between communicative behaviour and other sorts of intelligent behaviour.

That consideration is central to the work of Jerome Bruner. He goes so far (1975) as to discount the preoccupation with the learning of syntactic rules that dominated investigation in the 1960s as an actual distortion of our understanding of the process of language acquisition, and supports the view that a truer appreciation of what goes on is to be gained by looking closely at the early interaction between mothers and their young children. In particular he recommends that we should attend to the discourse features of that interaction. He instances as examples the use by English-speaking mothers of 'There!' to signal the start of a new activity and of 'Oh look!' to secure shared attention, followed at once by a comment on the subject of attention. Well before a child has reached the stage of producing readily intelligible utterances, he learns to expect that sequences will be ordered, not random. The child learns very early, according to Bruner, that references to place are regularly followed by mention of a feature, that the indication of an object is followed by a name or by the name of an act. Early language development is not, in his view, a matter of inferring rules from random, partial, and unhelpful data; rather, it is a process of learning to take part in meaningful discourse. In the earliest stages the child is a participant whose role is much more limited and less demanding than it will later become. Bruner observes that 'the mother is almost always the agent of the action; the child the recipient or experiencer' (p. 13). If a subordinate, responding role is a normal condition of the process by which language is acquired, it is entirely natural that children typically enter school supposing that just such a role will continue to be theirs in relation to these unknown adults who take over some aspects of parental function. It is a well-grounded expectation and as a rule it is abundantly confirmed. That teachers make the decisions, bear the responsibility, and do most of the talking, most of the time, is evident. Most children accept this state of affairs, and do not challenge it. How long the initial asymmetry should persist is another question altogether, of course, and one that is pertinent to a whole range of educational concerns.

Those issues that emerged in the 1970s — the shift from the concept of the language-acquiring child as 'a little linguist' to that of the developing baby as a participant in situated conversational interaction, the interest in the realisation of meaning in gesture and intonation and vocalisations other than speech, the concern with the involvement of the immediate family in the process by which communicative competence is acquired — all these are represented in M.A.K. Halliday's very detailed study of the acquisition of meaning by his son (1973 and 1975).

In one respect at least, his is a highly traditional study. It concentrates upon a single child growing up in the analyst's own family, and offering him virtually unlimited opportunities to observe and to check observation. Of course there is no ordinary sense in which such an upbringing could be considered 'typical'. None the less, there is an implicit assumption that what is exceptional is not fundamental, and while Nigel's situation may have been unique (very few children indeed have for parents two linguists, each having a distinguished international reputation) the processes of his language acquisition were not unrepresentative, nor, except in so far as they were closely observed and interpreted, is there any reason to suppose they were even unusual. What was observed and recorded, rather briefly in the 1973 papers, and in more detail in *Learning How to Mean* (1975), was that Nigel controlled at a very early stage a system quite different from that of the adults who took care of and interacted with him, but interpretable by them. The initial meaning system had very few elements; it was a pre-linguistic rather than a linguistic system, in which particular sounds and particular patterns of intonation were consistently associated with meanings which, within the small, attentive and sympathetic circle of the immediate family, could be understood and responded to. At this early stage, Nigel's system had meaning and sound, semantic and phonological components, but it had no level of form, no grammar. Then, with remarkable suddenness, and simultaneously, he acquired the elements of a grammatical system and the capacity for interactive dialogue, and was out of the pre-linguistic stage, in which he had got hold of the elements of what it is to mean, and was launched upon the acquisition of English as his mother tongue, and the immensely more varied meanings it would make available to him. At this critical point of initial approach to the adult system, language had two major functions for Nigel, one of them labelled the active function, the other, the pragmatic. A third, the imaginative function, was present in a role subsidiary to the other two. The contrasts between and among the functions were intonationally marked; they were prototypes of the functions that Nigel's adult English would eventually have. Their development occurred during and as a result of the interactive processes between the baby growing into childhood and his immediate family — processes that occupied most of his waking time. At the conclusion of the longer and more detailed of the two studies, Halliday discusses the significance of his observations up to that point in the still incomplete process:

Meaning is at the same time both a component of social action and a symbolic representation of the structure of social action. The semiotic structure of the environment, the ongoing social activity, the roles and statuses, and the interactional channels, both determines the meanings exchanged and is created by and formed out of them. This is why we understand what is said, and are able to fill out the condensations and unpeel the layers of projection. (*Learning How to Mean*, p. 143)

The clear implication is that the constraints on language that are present in specific situations affect it, not just in superficial ways, but fundamentally. If this is so, then it becomes a little less difficult to understand how it is that what very young speakers say should generally, though with the mistakes and misunderstandings usually associated with early learning, be recognised by those who hear them as appropriate, sensible, suitable to the context.

The Bristol project: Language at home and at school

Where studies focus upon a single child, or a small number of children, the questions at issue have to relate to what it is that some children do, and what may be the theoretical implications of what can be observed. The number, the variety, and the intrinsic interest of these studies has not made them centrally interesting to teachers of the youngest age group, and while this is, I believe, something to be regretted, and, if at all possible, to be changed, it is not hard to find reasons for the general neglect of linguistically based studies by those for whom educational concerns are paramount. Close observation of very small numbers of individuals, often of individuals growing up in unusually favourable circumstances, cannot readily provide a basis for the sort of informed decision-making on which improvements in the quality of institutional education depends. For someone concerned to find such a principled basis, the important question is not what occurs and may be observed, but, in terms of language development, what constitutes the normal range, and, what are the environmental conditions favourable to language development and amenable, at any rate in principle, to deliberate intervention.

The work of Gordon Wells and his associates in the Language at Home and at School project (based at the Research Unit of the Bristol University Institute of Education) is exceptional in several respects that make it appropriate to say something about it at the conclusion of this chapter. It is, like the studies discussed above, linguistically motivated. The work is seen as a contribution to our understanding of the processes by which language in general, and English in particular, is acquired. Those at work on it do however acknowledge, in the long term, a commitment to the improvement of educational provision. The age range studied is unusually long; at the start of the ten-year programme the youngest children were only 15 months old, and the oldest, at its conclusion were 7, and about to leave the primary for the junior school. The sample is, by contrast with other studies, very large; 128 boys and girls were selected from an initially much larger number, and chosen so as to secure an even distribution between the sexes and across the social spectrum. Children growing up to be bilingual were excluded, as were those whose acquisition of language would be affected by any sort of physical or mental handicap. The data collection from the children at home consists of audio recordings of language spoken by each child and heard by him. Each recording is of ninety seconds' duration, made intermittently over a twenty-four hour period. The recordings were controlled (with the consent of the family taking part) by a timing device which ensured that though the family knew that recordings were being made, they did not know exactly when the machine was in operation. The result is recorded data much closer to the ideal of spontaneously occurring unmonitored speech than any that had previously been assembled. The classroom data made use of black and white video recording. In terms of quantity, and quality, and longitudinal character, this is exceptional data — and it was manageable only because it was planned from the start to be computer-assisted, computer-stored, and to be accessible to researchers other than those taking part in the original project. At the time of writing, the data collection is complete. Substantial samples have been given limited publication. The design, the intentions and the interim progress of the project have been made known in a sequence of publications. It is clear that the results, the full discussion, and the conclusions, still eagerly awaited, will be uniquely important, and that we can look forward to a more fully informed discussion than has so far been possible of a range of questions important to parents and teachers and (to quote James Britton) 'anyone who wants to listen with more understanding to children and adolescents and who has for any reason a concern for what becomes of them'. These questions include what, in relation to language acquisition, constitutes the range of 'normality', how the intonation patterns of English are learned, whether the order of events in the learning process is constant for all children, or whether, conversely, they deploy a variety of distinct strategies to a single end. As the project has neared completion one overriding question — what are the experiences that facilitate or hinder acquisition of the mother tongue at home and early success at school? — has emerged into prominence and a clear indication of the position taken up has been made in advance of a complete account. Its direction is suggested by a question posed in a paper in which Wells and Montgomery (1981) present the developed analytic model they applied to their collection of data: 'Can some of the differences between children in the rate of initial language learning ... be accounted for by differences in the quality of the linguistic interaction they experience?' They indicate some of the factors that may determine the quality of that interaction, recalling an earlier description (Ellis and Wells, 1980) of the characteristically dissimilar ways in which adults address children they perceive as 'quick' or 'slow'. Those that adults perceive as intelligent and rapidly developing get more adult acknowledgment of what they offer, more instructions from adults, more verbal notice both of solitary and shared activities. These are differences that have to do with the child's character as the adult perceives it, but there seem to be differences also that have to do with particular adults' preferred styles of interaction with children generally. Of these, Wells distinguishes (Wells, 1979) between what he calls a 'supportive' style, one that encourages initiatives in children, acknowledges their efforts, and asks for additions, but lets the child himself make the running, and what he calls a 'teaching' style, where the adult chooses the topics and asks questions, giving the child (even if he knows the answers) a rather limited range of possible response, and frequent experience of being evaluated by adult standards as inadequate. Of these two styles of interaction, the second, the one that requires the child to display what he knows and can do (in Wells's terms), or to produce responses for adult evaluation (in Sinclair and Coulthard's) is typically associated with early schooling. The first is, in the view of Wells and his colleagues, the more successful in assisting the child towards linguistic maturity, and while they acknowledge a function for both 'supporting' and 'teaching' strategies, they develop a clear preference for the first, suggesting that language development is less likely to prosper if a child has little experience of activity shared with an adult, and accompanied by the sort of talk that acknowledges his right to take part in the exchange, and supports and extends his (often stumbling and hesitant) efforts to assert that right. Of course there can be all sorts of reasons why an individual child may not get much experience of that sort. By no means all adults, and not all parents, are able to take unforced pleasure in interaction with a newcomer to the speech community. Any of the pressures that bear upon families may preoccupy adults to the extent that interaction with children is less than frequent, lively, affectionate, and pleasurable to everyone concerned. Those concerned with this project are, however, anxious to dissociate themselves from the view that conditions of material poverty, and the unfavourable circumstances that belong with it, are in any direct or inevitable way associated with delayed, unsatisfactory language development and subsequent educational failure. They are at pains to cite examples from their data of positive and lively interaction going on in families on very low incomes. They are opposed to the notion of 'language deprivation' with its implication of an intellectual poverty trap from which only a minority of the exceptionally gifted and exceptionally lucky can hope to escape. This idea is widely prevalent, and so important in itself and in its effects that it needs to be separately discussed, and in the context of the educationally motivated studies with which it is primarily associated.

This chapter has been concerned with the changing landscape of the study of the language children acquire at home and bring to school. The continuing factor has been the conviction among linguists that this study is fundamental to our understanding of the nature, the structure, and the functions of language. What has changed since the start of the 1960s has been the extent to which this study is abstracted from practical, and particularly from educational, concerns. It retains its autonomy, but is less self-contained. It has not proved possible to restrict the study to the production and understanding of speech, disregarding those sorts of communicative behaviour that precede speech and continue to accompany and supplement it. Nor has it been possible to concentrate, to the virtual exclusion of all else, upon that rather short period when the learning of the grammatical rules of the mother tongue goes on most noticeably and rapidly, nor to overlook the varieties of setting and circumstance in which language acquisition occurs. One effect of such an extension of interest is that specialists in other areas — sociology, social anthropology, education — are currently involved with linguists in debate, and their papers appear at conferences and in collections, contributing to discussion and offering contrasting perspectives, often critical of linguists' bias towards the verbal element in the communication process. Waterson and Snow (1978), in an editorial introduction to one of a number of important collections of papers, identify five significant departures from the assumptions and directions of the previous decade. They see meaning and function, the semantic and the pragmatic components of language, in the central, dominating position formerly occupied by syntax; the social context of language acquisition is recognised as crucially important; the traditional concerns of psychologists – the development of cognitive and perceptual abilities – are recognised as the subject of studies that linguists cannot ignore. They see the question that assumed fundamental importance in the 1960s – what can possibly be innate? – not abandoned, but reinterpreted, and finding a place within a generally broader enquiry, that examines a broader age range, with a changed emphasis that entails 'recognition that what and how the child communicates is primary, and enables the child to learn syntactic structures' (Waterson and Snow, 1978, p. xvi).

The relevance of linguistically motivated studies to educational concerns is, in consequence of such shifts, much more evident than it was. A convergence of interest and concern is apparent where formerly the study of a various and complicated topic was unevenly divided amongst investigators who approached it from different positions and employed different methodologies in pursuit of dissimilar purposes. When, in the late 1960s, the team based at Birmingham began work on examining the discourse of classrooms their primary concern was with strictly linguistic questions; what is discourse structure like in English? what is the primary unit of discourse? what are the rules for allowing some combinations and disallowing others? They chose to focus on the discourse of classrooms not because they expected as a result to improve the quality of what went on there (though they never lost sight of the possibility that by making an understanding of discourse processes available to teachers they might, indirectly, and in the long term, achieve something in that respect), but rather because classroom interaction seemed to be more orderly and purposeful than many other sorts of verbal interchange, was reasonably easy of access, and had already, when they began work, been the subject of a very large number indeed of educationally motivated studies. Some of these, and the traditions developed within them and extended into the 1970s, are brought into focus in the next chapter. In contrast with work on the acquisition of language done by linguists, and concerned centrally with what is common to all children in process of acquiring their mother tongue, studies having their principled basis in education as a discipline have emphasised what for any educational system (and any teacher of a class) constitutes a problem – that there are few assumptions to be made about what children can do at entry to school. They vary in what they have learned, in the rate and in the success with which they have learned and they continue to do so.

2

Varieties of language use among newcomers to the classroom

Like the last this chapter is concerned with recent studies, but with studies of language use during the years of schooling rather than with the processes of language acquisition. The motivation too is different; it is, in broad terms, the conviction that educational experience is capable of being significantly improved. For many children it is neither happy nor, in measurable terms, successful. Many teachers, too, are less than fully effective. Given the centrality of language to the educational process it is reasonable to think that the study of language use, in class-rooms, by pupils and by teachers, may furnish the insights necessary to direct successful intervention.

Several distinct traditions are involved, and the recognition of this determines the way in which this chapter is organised. There is a central concern, of long standing, that stems from a predominantly American preoccupation with teacher-effectiveness. Where, as in American society and others like it, including our own, education is general, and is a public charge, then the inability of some children to make use of it is a matter of public concern and rises to peaks of anxiety. There is another tradition, newer and based in the United Kingdom, that brings to bear upon spoken and written texts, produced in classrooms in response to educational requirements, the critical seriousness and sensitivity associated with the study of English literature, and finds in the language of teachers an element of paradox. This is a recurring theme, and several routes lead to it. What is usually regarded as 'good' language use on the part of teachers – lucid, confident, articulate, informed – does not seem to produce similar qualities in pupils' language use. On the contrary, there is evidence of a disquieting sort, that it actually hampers children's language development. Interchange between each of these traditions and those concerned primarily with the nature of the process by which language is acquired has in the past been slight and infrequent. Linguistically motivated and educationally motivated studies have been

pursued in partial isolation from each other, and there have only recently
been points of convergence. The work of Bernstein is such an exception. It has given rise to a programme of intervention; it is conceived in
broadly sociolinguistic terms. It has, in addition been very widely dis-
seminated and highly influential among teachers and those administrators who make educational decisions. The concluding section of this
chapter raises some general issues about the relation between studies
that relate to classroom language, and the observable processes of
innovation and change.

Educationally motivated studies of classroom interaction

Just how impressive is the quantity of educationally motivated research relating to classroom language is apparent from surveys of that
literature, of which the earliest, Medley and Mitzel (1963) has been
updated by others less comprehensive, but including reference to British
as well as to American work prepared by Wragg and by Brown (both in
Chanan and Delamont, 1975). It is not only the evidence of industry
and tenacity that is impressive. There is a clear consensus, too, of a
widespread conviction that successful educational outcomes depend
heavily on satisfactory interaction, predominantly verbal interaction,
between teachers and their classes. The quality of talk that teachers
initiate and sustain is for that reason of paramount importance. Further,
there is an assumption that quality is not solely dependent on something so arbitrary as individual flair. Classroom interaction is in principle analysable. It can be described. Effects can be related to causes;
effectiveness can be measured, and (in principle at any rate) can be
increased. The effect of that conviction is the design, by individual
researchers, of systems for coding and analysing successive classroom
events, of which that associated with the name of N.A. Flanders is the
best known and the most widely and variously employed. The number
of these coding systems is so extremely large as to make them a study
in themselves (surveyed by Simon and Boyer, 1973; and Rosenshine
and Furst, 1973). Educationally oriented research in classroom language takes a broad and inclusive view of what is important, is (almost
by definition) sensitive to the importance of the immediate and the
wider situation of language use, and takes into account all sorts of non-
vocal and non-verbal communicative activity — gestures, looks and
expressions, and positions taken up by individuals relative to one
another, for example. There is an assumption though, that talk is in

some sense *central* to the whole process of interaction and representative of it. Educationists and linguists alike take this representative character of language in communication to be intuitively evident, not to be challenged, and not in need of justification. An inclusive view of what is important in classroom interaction is more readily compatible with linguists' recent, and current, concern with the acquisition of communicative competence in a context of language use, than with their earlier and narrower focus on the learning of the operation of syntactic rules. The overriding impetus to educational research is concern for the quality of pupils' educational experience and teachers' professional expertise, and with ways in which these can be improved. These are concerns shared by some, but not all, linguists. The principle that linguists observe, frame hypotheses, test, and reformulate and avoid offering, let alone insisting upon, advice, is still well established, but is increasingly regarded as a privileged position that must be sustained if premature and over-optimistic judgments are to be avoided, but cannot be continued indefinitely. Educational and sociolinguistic researchers alike share concerns that were excluded from those earlier language acquisition studies that focused on the universal character of the process. These include the many dimensions of difference among children engaged in learning to talk and to understand. It is important though not to underestimate the actual divergences of approach and method and assumption that characterise the two traditions. Of these divergences, one seems to me to have had less than its due of attention, and to be inescapable by anybody who brings sociolinguistic interests to bear upon a close involvement with children and teachers. Linguists are sensitised by everything they know and do to the complexity of human language. The literature of the 1960s discussed in the preceding chapter is full of expressions of something like awe at the perfectly ordinary young child's rapid mastery of his mother tongue. Later work has been occasionally critical of these, the sense of language acquisition as a marvel has steadied and cooled, but it has by no means been eroded. There is still the sense that normal children of school age, including those least successful in educational terms, have already demonstrated convincingly their ability to learn, and are already in possession of a substantial amount of operational knowledge. Educationists perceive children differently, and such a view as unrealistic, in terms of what schools and society require. For them the keenest stimulus to enquiry is offered by the children who disappoint, fail to respond to what is offered, do not make the progress teachers expect, and emerge at the end of a decade of exposure to full-time education barely literate, uninformed, incurious.

Where educational priorities determine the character of investigation it is common to find linguistic assumptions which are not made explicit. It is often assumed not only that the extent of educational failure, by children, in relation to the norms institutionalised in the educational system is substantial, but that this failure is capable in principle of being significantly reduced (Bereiter and Engelmann, 1966; Hannam, Smyth and Stephenson, 1976). It is a matter of finding the right teaching strategies for populations whose observed failure is attributed to slow or inadequate language development, leading to missed educational opportunities that cannot (without intentional and expensive intervention) be repeated or replaced. It is simply assumed that slow development can be accelerated, and impoverished learning made good, by providing a modified environment and a different range of experiences. The nature of this provision as a rule consists in arranging that situations occur repeatedly in which those uses of language in which pupils are deficient, those in which they rarely or never engage spontaneously, are required to be demonstrated in the hearing of a teacher. They must make a response that can be evaluated. The provision amounts to a sharp increase in the number of occasions offered for display. These are assumptions still widely shared, but they have not gone unchallenged. Studies have been available for some time that call them in question at least to the extent of indicating that alternative strategies are possible (Horner and Gussow, 1972; Mischler, 1972, for example).

While certainly it is the case that any study that employs a system for categorising classroom utterances may be said to imply an orderly character for the processes of interaction, it is still true to say that few educationally motivated studies have given more than incidental consideration to the discourse structure. To this generalisation, however, there is an exception, notable both for the scope of its design and for the fact that it had no immediate successors. This was the study carried out by Bellack, Kliebard, and their associates, on a topic generalisable beyond the secondary schools in which they obtained their data. They posed this question: of the various teaching styles teachers employ, which best facilitates learning, judged by the educational criteria commonly in use? In the course of their investigation the team found it necessary to design a model of classroom interaction, and to apply to their texts a coding system derived from it. They excluded everything except the verbal component from consideration. They were influenced, not by current work in the acquisition of language, but by Wittgenstein's seminal work in linguistic philosophy. They quote his famous saying, 'the meaning of a word is its use in language', and make use of his image of language use as a game constituted by the conventions players agree to accept. They set themselves to identify and account for the varied functions of classroom language — giving and obeying orders, putting forward and testing guesses, making believe, telling jokes, inventing and telling stories. In the process they design a model of discourse which is hierarchically arranged. Four sorts of *move* (structuring, soliciting, responding, directing) combine in two sorts of *cycle*, and from this model they were able to develop a coding system that could be applied to their extensive body of text independently of their other measure of learning and of attitude change. They reached unsurprising, but well founded and carefully documented, conclusions: teachers are more verbally active in lessons than are pupils; constraints on what may be said by teachers and by pupils are well understood and rarely challenged; teachers' preferred styles are generally stable; making and explaining statements accounts for rather more than half of teachers' utterances. (Only the last of these is, in my observation, specific to teachers' interaction with secondary pupils.) Sinclair and Coulthard pay general tribute to work that, had it come to the attention of the Birmingham team at an early and critical stage of the development of their model, might have been more directly influential than it was. The central feature of that work, the serious, though as Bellack, Kliebard and their associates were the first to point out, no more than partially successful effort to establish relations between describable styles of interaction and outcomes in terms of learning has still no successor.

Interaction studies of the 1950s and 1960s are predominantly teacher-centred. It is not just that the teacher is a key participant. Where the intention is to modify interaction, to improve its quality judged by educational criteria, it is teachers who must be addressed and persuaded to modify what they do in response to research findings. The channels of communication between researchers and teachers, though their restrictions are often deplored, are available. Books and papers are read, conferences are attended, teachers are interested in understanding the nature of their own professional activity and in sharpening their skills. With that said it has to be acknowledged that these studies are associated with a model of learning that represents knowledge as material for transmission, from teacher to pupil, from the older generation to the younger. Such a model of learning, while it is not universal, and is currently subjected to a good deal of criticism, is still dominant, is deeply embedded in the structure of classroom discourse, and is, for reasons to which I shall want to return, very resistant to change.

The paradox of teacher talk

Recent approaches to the study of classroom language include two groups of studies within an overall educational framework. Of these, that which is sociological in its motivation, associated with the authoritative figure of Basil Bernstein, has been powerfully influential among teachers and educational decision-makers. The other, associated with education considered as an academic discipline, and particularly with the teaching of English, is interesting for another reason. The teaching of the mother tongue in English schools gives increasing prominence, as pupils grow older, to literary studies. Sixth-form studies, for the most part the prestigious and personally rewarding aspect of the job for secondary English teachers, are dominated by the development of appreciation by pupils of masterpieces of English writing and of the ability to verbalise a critical response. That is the background of a group of recent studies of the language use of much younger, much less advanced pupils, written and presented at a deliberately non-theoretical level, and made deliberately accessible to a wide and serious general public. David Holbrook is in this respect a pioneer, and makes a persuasive case for the relation between personality development and the later stages of the acquisition of the mother tongue in *English for Maturity* (1961), and for the significance of this relationship for the least educationally successful pupils, in *English for the Rejected* (1964). Other names, those of Douglas Barnes and his associates, James Britton, the Rosens, have become prominent more recently. Nobody questions the need to close the gap, frequently deplored, between academic researchers and those who make and implement educational decisions or who simply are interested in children's language development, and, more specifically, their development in school settings. What makes this tradition of study interesting, and indeed challenging to me, is that these authors engage in the study of spoken and written language independently of linguistics. Holbrook regards the inclusion of the subject in the professional preparation of teachers as a wasteful and harmful expenditure of energy and time. Since linguistic study, however it is undertaken, does undoubtedly involve very considerable investment of time and energy, the burden of demonstrating that it is a proper and a necessary concern of teachers, that it does actually repay, in terms of professional insight, the effort it requires, clearly devolves upon those who believe that this is so, and who study and teach and write from that conviction. There is no such compulsion to deprecate studies undertaken from a contrary conviction of course, on the contrary their effect has been, I believe, to reflect and inform a significant and very desirable shift in public and professional opinion. Authors working in this tradition have assembled and transcribed records of spoken text in which children have participated, and written text produced in educational settings and in response to teachers' initiatives. Text that was formerly disregarded as the disposable by-product of the educational process has been identified as deserving of serious consideration. One effect of that attention is that it is now almost certainly easier than it was for a child to speak and be heard, to write and be read. This is not to say that most children are not passive and more or less attentive listeners during the greater part of their experience of schooling. The work has contributed significantly to the general recognition among teachers of the unique status English has as at the same time the subject and the means of study. It has been influential in great part because there has been minimal reference to linguistic or educational theory. The report by Rosen and Rosen (1973) of the Schools Council Project on Language Development in the Primary School goes further, claiming that absence as a merit, as if the intention to explain in principled terms were actually inimical to the qualities of feeling, the sensitivity and warmth of response that is the precondition of good work. If the conventions of report writing had permitted, these authors would have preferred to have presented instead a selection from taped texts. Their brief, to seek out and study examples of good practice in classroom interaction, allowed them to collect 'lucky random trophies . . . on raiding expeditions'. These trophies, examples of the spoken English that can occur in classrooms where gifted and imaginative teachers share the authors' conviction that children experience vividly the reality of learning in minimally constrained talk to a sympathetic listener, comprise, with commentary, the most interesting part of the report. Elsewhere (for example by Britton, 1970, and by Martin, 1971) the reader is invited to share the writers' infectious enthusiasm for the qualities of freshness, vitality, and unexpectedness that characterise excerpts from oral and written composition produced by children. These are selected for quotation (they illustrate what children can do and make no claim to typicality or representativeness) and are sometimes discussed in terms of explicit comparison between children's production and adult poetry. Such a comparison effectively suggests that the traditional preoccupation of teachers with the degree to which pupils approximate towards adult standards in spelling, punctuation, and the production of grammatically well-formed sentences, may distort response, and get in the way of appreciation of what the writers mean and can say. There is no answer to the question how far, and for whom *are* these preoccupations important? do they deserve the pride of place they have in the past received? if not, then how, if at all, are the majority of pupils to assimilate them? Questions relating to the importance of spontaneous and expressive language use are assumed to have been already answered, and the reply to the enquiry about the conditions of its occurrence is couched in terms of the sympathetic, but not uncritical, encouragement, and the varied stimulation provided by gifted individual teachers. Explanation of how language functions in classroom settings has to be sought elsewhere. The effect of these studies is to recommend to teachers a high degree of reticence, a willingness to listen to what pupils have to say, to forgo some part of their traditional dominance in favour of much more subtle and indirect control — a kind of control that is, in any except unusually favourable circumstances, very much more difficult to secure and to maintain. Put broadly the indication is that teachers talk *too much*, that the effect of their adult fluency and confidence is to swamp pupils' often hesitant efforts to find language for an incompletely realised meaning. They do this so frequently and constantly that, far from offering their pupils a helpful model of adult language use, they succeed chiefly in reinforcing children's feelings of inadequacy, and making coherent and articulate speech less likely. Traditionally 'effective' teachers, confident by disposition and training, brisk, clear and articulate speakers, may actually inhibit language development in pupils.

This is not an encouraging paradox, and it is hard to see that it can be resolved except in terms of understanding of the interactive, reciprocal character of situated discourse. It is a pointer to one part of the case for sociolinguistically motivated studies of classroom language. They are accountable, in ways that can be described (though they may be more or less direct), to linguistic models. Where that relationship can be shown to be fragile or distorted the studies concerned do not require or deserve serious consideration and should be discarded. They do not depend, in any significant degree, upon shared taste between writer and reader. Given that the purposes of such studies include the attainment of insights that are cumulative, and contribute something, if only a little, to our developing understanding of large issues, and to the possibility of making decisions from a wider range of options, these seem to me to be serious claims.

The work and influence of Bernstein

Of the influences affecting teachers' responses to the language children use, none has been so persuasive as Bernstein's. More than any other single influence, his is responsible for the current educational ortho-doxy that language use in school is crucially important because there is a causal relationship between pupils' understanding and use of language and their educational, and subsequent occupational, success. That work is known not just as a result of publication, but by a process of dis-semination that includes courses of study at different levels of sophisti-cation. It is not a matter for surprise that initial ideas, subjected to pro-cesses of development and change, should be those most firmly estab-lished. What is perceived, and what is retained could not unfairly be characterised like this: failure in school is, very often, the result of poverty of language experience in the home. This is associated with relative material poverty, and is endemic in homes where 'conversation' – in the sense of unhurried interchange on a wide variety of topics, not all of them immediate – is no part of the established culture, and where the resulting void, if it is filled at all, is filled with broadcast sound. Such an upbringing results in a sort of generalised defect rather like the vitamin deficiency consequent on an insufficient, unsuitable diet. Schools can do almost nothing to counter this state of affairs, and res-ponsibility for the generally disappointing and unhappy response of urban working-class children to what is offered them lies elsewhere. It must be added that this represents a view from which (in 1970 and on several occasions since) Bernstein has repeatedly dissociated himself. His major tenet is that language is a principal means by which cultures are transmitted between the generations; that this is true not only of those cultures remote from our own, that have traditionally been the subject of anthropological studies, but also of subcultures associated with social class divisions, in our own society and others like it. Institu-tions, including educational institutions, embody norms and values that are not those of the working-class pupils who enter them. These tenets have been explored and extended, but not modified in essential ways, during the long duration (ten years) of the project Bernstein directed. With them goes this implication: that the language of teachers and pupils in classroom settings is particularly interesting since that is where different subcultures meet, inescapably, regularly, and over a long time. That part of the transmission process is deliberately set up, and for that reason, it is potentially modifiable. The studies of classroom language to which Bernstein's views gave such powerful impetus concentrate, predictably, on a single dimension of variation, that which is social class-related, on observable contrasts in the language use of working-class and middle-class groups, and the thrust of the enquiry has been the question which, of the various options available to speakers of English, are habitually selected by members of each group? The options taken into account are either lexical or syntactic. The term used by Bernstein for the range of choices habitual to working-class speakers, *restricted code*, is not intended to relate to the accent regionally or socially marked, which is for most middle-class speakers, including teachers, their most immediately recognisable feature. The contrasting term, the *elaborated code*, for the range of options, the code to which middle-class speakers, and only they, have access is by now so well established, and the pair of terms so constantly in use in any debate about the relation of language to educability, that regret for the value judgment implied in the terms themselves is not sufficient to secure change. Bernstein has stressed the positive value of the sort of encoding of meaning that he calls restricted; it is the elliptical, inexplicit use of language that is natural to intimate and warm interchange, in contrast to the elaborated code, which, by its very explicitness, often functions to maintain social distance. However, if, as typically happens, some children bring to school fluency in a use of language that depends for its communicative function upon shared knowledge and shared assumptions, and if others arrive already accustomed to understand that other people often do not know what to the speaker is entirely familiar, and that language is for reaching out towards new experience, as well as for asserting and confirming that which is already known, then it is difficult to imagine *any* educational process to which language is central, in which the second group will not have a significant advantage over the first. And in general that advantage is retained, since the language differences seem not to be eroded by the shared experience of schooling. Further, the advantage of a successful start is cumulative; more opportunities are made available to the pupil who is perceived by his teacher as responsive and bright; more demands are made on him. The distance between the children on the 'top table' and those on the 'bottom table' in the reception classroom is more likely to widen than to close as they move through the system into junior and secondary education.

Bernstein's view is that here we have a substantial explanation of what is not in dispute — that the children of working-class families do less well than those of middle-class families on the ordinary measures of educational attainments. At the end of the process they leave full-time education as soon as they can, minimally qualified, to take up (at best) jobs where prospects are poor, and maximum earning powers are reached early. Where unemployment is high, they bear the brunt of it. They, in their turn, raise families of children who reach school as poorly equipped linguistically as their parents were. It is a persuasive argument addressed to a problem of urgent public concern; it has been a highly influential one. It does of course depend upon the premise that access to some language functions, notably those that serve inter-personal communication among people who have large areas of experience in common, and not to others, actually *is* typical of those groups whose educational and occupational status assigns them to the working class. If those who are the losers in an educational system essentially competitive, are, so to speak, retrospectively designated restricted code users, then what we have is not *explanation*. It is as if it were asserted that the losers in a race are those inferior to the winners in terms of speed and stamina. At best we could claim no more than a valuable contribution to our understanding of the conditions of educational success.

Intervention programmes (on both sides of the Atlantic) have looked to Bernstein's work for support for their underlying supposition that, if it could be arranged to extend to young working-class children those sorts of language experience which, at entry to school, middle-class children seem already to have had, and to have learned from, then the two groups would be able to compete on equal terms. The 'social handicap' that impeded the first group would have been removed. There would be better use made overall of an educational system that represents a substantial investment on the part of society. Pupils of working-class origin would no longer be, as they are at present, under-represented among those groups proceeding to higher education and the professions. Even among strong advocates of intervention there are occasional signs of uneasiness at these assumptions and they have been vigorously challenged. In an influential paper, several times reprinted, Labov (1969) demonstrates that the language employed by working-class pupils in what they perceive as test situations is, relative to that of pupils of middle-class origin, informal, elliptical, inexplicit, and, in general terms, sparse and reluctant. His *description* of the variety of English they employ is not very dissimilar from Bernstein's. His *interpretation*, however, is quite different, since it is couched not in terms of the language functions controlled by these children, which are inadequate for an important range of educational purposes, but in terms of their different perceptions of these purposes. Working-class pupils, in his view, perceive testing procedures as in their nature punitive, as assertions of power by those who have it already, manipulative in intention and in purpose. While it is reasonable for teachers to regard such perceptions as seriously mistaken, it can hardly be claimed that they are either irrational or unfounded. Further, Labov contests the view that working-class language is inherently unsuited to a number of functions that are important to the educational process, and he demonstrates by quotation that arguments of some subtlety, relating to abstract propositions, may perfectly well be expressed in the stigmatised variety of English employed by black working-class speakers. He argues that, conversely, the use of a variety of English that enjoys high social prestige can secure favourable attention for the repetitive expression of trivialities. (This last, at least, has never been in doubt.) It is a convincing demonstration that the supposed unfitness for educational purposes of socially stigmatised varieties of English is a questionable assumption. It remains, however, in educational circles, an extremely powerful one.

An intervention programme, employing the findings so as to improve the educational chances of young working-class children, was a condition of support for the project in Primary Language and Socialisation that Bernstein directed. Those who worked on it (principally Gahagan and Gahagan, 1972) concerned themselves closely with spoken interaction in home and school settings, though they did not, as Coulthard (1975) pointed out, take what seemed, a decade after they started work, the obvious next step of examining the structure of the discourse created there. That does seem now a necessary means of testing the belief that between the language of middle-class children and the expectations of their teachers, there is an educationally productive match that just does not obtain between those same teachers and their working-class pupils. The title of the report in which the Gahagans describe their work, *Talk Reform*, well indicates the thrust of the intervention programme for which, under Bernstein's general direction, they were responsible (and illustrates too the sort of optimistic assertion of the possibility of rapid and radical improvement that linguists warily avoid).

Their brief was to design and test a programme that could be carried out in an ordinary primary school, with minimal disturbance to its usual work, and with little special provision, either in material terms or in terms of special training undertaken by teachers. They were to diagnose and amend that sort of language use by children that was not educationally useful. Their programme was related, though not in a very specific way, to some of those functions which Halliday (1969) posited as typically already within the control of children at entry to school. In the event they seem to have perceived their task in psychological rather than in linguistic terms. They designed exercises and activities to encourage in children a longer concentration span, more detailed recall, and more exact discrimination among sounds, and they hoped as a result to accelerate the development of just those characteristics which may reasonably be supposed to be the prerequisites of successful learning. They characterise – inevitably since they were committed to working within the Bernstein paradigm – the language their subjects spontaneously use as restricted code, and the language of their teachers, which they must become familiar with, as elaborated code. They offer (as Bernstein himself does) constructed examples, legitimately enough, in order to clarify these distinctions, and subsequently treat these, not as hypothetical examples to be tested against the evidence of actually occurring text, but as evidence for the validity and significance of the concepts they were designed to illustrate. This is a criticism that has been made several times, and not just of the Gahagans' work, but more generally of the project directed by Bernstein. More is involved than a criticism of the methodology. Rather, those who are critical of the polar opposition indicated by the terms restricted and elaborated code (for example, Labov, 1969; and Williams, 1970, in the US; Coulthard, 1969; Rosen, 1972; and Stubbs, 1976 and 1980, in the UK) are in agreement that there is in this important and influential work a general failure to engage with the realities of spontaneously occurring, informal, spoken English text. Of course the criticisms have not gone unanswered and Bernstein has, in a paper originally addressed to an audience at Teachers' College, Columbia, and reprinted under the title 'A critique of the concept of compensatory education', rejected out of hand the simplest and most damaging negative inference from his work – that not much can be expected of the majority of urban working-class children. In a careful foreword to a collection of papers relating to this area Halliday (1973) attempts to disentangle the actual significance of Bernstein's work from those simplified distortions of it that are current among an interested, concerned and serious public that includes many teachers. At the conclusion of his discussion of 'the significance of Bernstein's work for educational theory' he says that the pupil, the school, and society itself require a broadening of the concept of meaning and of language, adding that Bernstein's work has signally contributed to bringing about just such a modification:

> Language is central to Bernstein's theory; but in order to understand the place it occupies, it is necessary to think of language as meaning rather than of language as structure. (p. 107)

That work is to be valued he argues, first, because it is addressed to a fundamental question — that of the educational underfunctioning of working-class children relative to those better off, a difference that can no longer be wholly explained in terms of relative lack of opportunity; second, because it attempts explanation of the process of cultural transmission; third, because the answers are couched not only in social terms, but in terms broadly sociolinguistic. It is regrettable, and not inevitable, that its dissemination in popular terms should have seemed to confirm and authorise the sorts of prejudice that determine just those expectations that in their turn partially determine performance.

Of the work pursued and carried out independently of Bernstein, which yet fully acknowledges his influence, that associated with the name of Joan Tough has been the most influential, and the most substantial. Her concern, over a period of time, has been to establish just what is the nature of the underlying disadvantage that depresses the attainment of working-class children. The terms in which the questions are formulated are informed by Bernstein's work. Social class is seen not as the single determinant, but as the major determinant, of success and failure. Tough's work is more than an intervention programme: action research would be a more accurate description. It has immediate applications, and since as a matter of policy she involved large numbers of teachers at every stage, those applications have been widely acknowledged. The overall purpose is to enquire how the verbal interchange that occurs between teachers and their young pupils can be made educationally more productive. That work began in 1965 with a study of new entrants to schooling, and was extended at the completion of its first phase to allow for the sampling techniques developed to be applied to children of 7 and 11. Large samples of naturally occurring speech constituted the data used. Although she made use of grammatical measures in examining the data, Tough's approach is primarily functional, and her contention is that the characteristic advantage enjoyed by middle-class children does not lie in their use of more complicated syntactic structures than working-class children of the same age typically employ. This is, so to speak, an accident or by-product. Rather, middle-class children employ more frequently and more readily some functions that language has for all children. This contention is supported by what has been several times observed — that working-class children *do* control functions that they rarely see reason to use spontaneously in educational settings, and it is not too difficult to elicit them, and demonstrate that this is so, as Labov convincingly did. Tough recognises that in the study of children's acquisition of communicative competence, control of function has to be the primary concern, and syntax, the level at which functions are realised, secondary. Her findings support the view that her middle-class subjects have, at entry to school, already become familiar with just those language functions that the educational process requires them to exercise.

She works with a model of language that identifies four *functions*: *directive, interpretive, projective, relational*. Each *function* comprises several, rather more specific *uses*, and each *use* is realised by a number of *strategies*. It is (like that of Bellack, Kliebard, *et al.* (see p. 32), and like that of Sinclair and Coulthard, 1975) a hierarchical model, and one that implies a recognition that a model of language must make claim to comprehensiveness. As Sinclair and Coulthard put it, unless it is possible to say something about *all* the data, nothing explanatory can be said about *any* of it. Tough says that nearly all of the utterances in her large sample were analysable in terms of this model, leaving no more than a small number of dubious or marginal cases. That seems like a strong claim, not just for the results obtained by the author, but for the use of her model by other people, having different purposes and dissimilar samples of data. The claim is however hedged by a puzzling degree of caution (in *The Development of Meaning*, 1977): 'It does not seem likely that the classification is exhaustive, or would be entirely appropriate for adult language' (p. 67), and the disclaimer prompts important questions: if it is *not* exhaustive, what additional functional categories, or what modifications to those already established, would be needed in order to secure exhaustiveness? If adult language functions are different, how do they differ, and what sort of developmental process is at work in bringing about the difference? The claim that the functions as they stand account for most of the utterances produced by young pupils has been authoritatively challenged. Wells (1977) applied the categories to a selection of comparable data obtained in the course of the Bristol project, and found them unsatisfactory in use. There are inherent limitations in the model. It offers no way of relating functions to discourse structure, and it does not indicate what the function-signalling devices of English are. The user of the model, the person, that is, attempting to apply the categories to data of his own, has to rely on his own internalised native speaker's knowledge of the ways in which in English, functions of language are realised in order to assign particular utterances to given categories and where two native speakers differ in their judgment, there is no principled way of resolving the difference. Where the task is successfully accomplished, as it was in the substantial excerpts cited and analysed in *The Development of Meaning* (ch. 7, p. 24 *et seq*.) the result is a brief functional description, utterance by utterance. In terms of the Bellack and Kliebard model it is description of the level of the *move*, while in Sinclair and Coulthard's, it is description at the level of the *act*. The description allows the author to show that particular functions occur with varying degrees of frequency between individual children at the same age, between the utterances of the same individual at different developmental stages, and between groups of children. This is entirely pertinent to her purpose, since for her, language is chiefly interesting as evidence of varying and developing cognitive strategies, and her overall design includes establishing a relation between characteristic strategies and social class, and demonstrating that these strategies may be more, or less, compatible with the expectations embodied in the educational system. It is a model designed to classify utterances, rather than to take account of the structures of which those utterances are part. That children generally, irrespective of social class, recognise turn-taking, understand that questions require answers and instructions require responses is acknowledged, but not pursued. For my purposes in examining the development (by children only a little older than Tough's youngest subjects) of the ability to interact with their teachers in appropriate and expected ways, the functional model developed in connection with this project was simply not suitable. A hierarchical model was needed, certainly, but with this indispensable condition — that its basic unit should be a discourse unit, not the utterance but the exchange, to which two participants contribute.

Much that has emerged from Tough's studies is, none the less, sympathetic, and experience in classrooms supports her conclusions and confirms their importance. She confirms by her findings the belief that many teachers, themselves fluent and articulate speakers, overwhelm young children's efforts with their talk. With the kindest intentions, sensitive as they are to the newcomer's need to be noticed, identified, reassured, and appreciated, they talk at him and round him, casting him always in a responding role, in which brief answers, uttered hesitantly, seem the only possible responses. Other people (Shields and Steiner, for instance, in their 1973 study) have come by a variety of routes to a similar conclusion, and the observation of teachers and others supports it. It would be difficult to contest Tough's persuasive recommendation that more various, more imaginative, and more professional approaches are required from teachers so as to demonstrate to children that there are, in educational settings, acceptable alternatives to the monosyllabic response. Where the problems are seen, as they are here, in broadly psychological terms explanation seems out of reach except in terms that are hardly plausible. While one may certainly suppose that teaching is a profession unlikely to attract naturally diffident individuals, it is clearly not the case that most teachers are naturally assertive and talkative people who would dominate conversation in any company.

The period of nearly total estrangement between studies motivated by educational concern and studies motivated by concern to understand the nature and function of language, seems to have coincided with the 1960s, and to have ended with the decade. Of course the priorities of the two groups continue to differ. The structure of discourse, as distinct from its functions, does seem to have been generally disregarded by educationists for whom the priority is the identification of the causes of less than adequate learning, that is, once understood, capable of improvement. If diagnosis and prescription are the goal, then there is always pressure of immediate need, and recommendation has priority over description.

Conservatism and innovation in classrooms

Any account, however brief and partial, of the development of our understanding of the differences between and among children in respect of linguistic insight and abilities to comprehend and to produce English as their mother tongue at entry to school, has to prompt the question how much in terms of change has actually been accomplished? Classrooms are notoriously conservative in their operation. While it is likely they are happier and freer places than they were, this change is attributable to many causes, and reflects changes in the way society generally believes children should be brought up. It is widely accepted that the rate of educational failure is high, that failure typically starts early, and that it is rarely reversed. Many children are unhappy, uncomprehending, and disorganised at school and this is a matter for widespread anxiety. That language is central to the learning process, and that educational success or failure are in some important sense related to language, has the status of an educational orthodoxy, in the face of which the belief, current well within living memory, that talking in class constituted a sort of educational original sin, has been long in retreat. (There are more than occasional rueful expressions of regret for the older style of classroom, where the teacher's voice held unquestioned sway, however.) These are changes of a profound sort. Research, educationally or linguistically motivated, has probably made its contribution to their distribution and acceptance.

Once orthodoxies are established, they have a vigorous life of their own, are held with conviction, and inform decisions, policies and expectations. The conviction that language differs between social classes, and that the variety typical of working-class children makes a disappointing response to educational experience probable is one such orthodoxy, no less influential because it is a matter of observation that by no means all teachers, perhaps not a majority, habitually use a 'BBC English', a standard English that is, with a 'received pronunciation'. The notion that 'language deficit' is widespread among urban working-class children is a commonplace. Where it is disowned in favour of the contrary assertion that no such value judgment is appropriate — working-class language simply is different — the assumption is still that the differences are of such a sort that they make educational success difficult and infrequent. Recognition of regional differences is of long standing, and the assumption has regularly been that where teacher and pupils do not share a regional variety, they will find some sort of workable accommodation that makes it possible for them to understand each other nearly all the time. Population changes in the last twenty years have challenged the assumption that it is normal and natural for children in this country to arrive at school speaking and understanding a variety of English not too dissimilar from the language of their teacher, and not too far removed from the language they will learn to read and write. This is not true, for example, of some children of Caribbean parents, speakers of an English that most teachers hear as underdeveloped, ungrammatical, and frequently unintelligible. Where they know that it is in fact neither of the first two, the barrier to understanding is still a reality. The presence in classrooms for the youngest children of some for whom English is not the first language is not a novelty either. The assumption has been that, though they would undoubtedly experience some feelings of strangeness in the initial weeks, they would quickly pick up the language from the teacher and, more significantly and more rapidly, from their English classmates. So strong was this belief that when, in the mid-1960s, much effort and experience was devoted to designing teaching methods and materials for what were then termed 'immigrant children' in the junior and secondary ranges, the youngest children were largely ignored, on the grounds that the infant classroom presented, without modification, an almost ideal language learning environment. Where, as is the case in a small minority of schools at present, speakers of languages not English constitute a *majority*, and only one or two of the total number share with their teacher English as a mother tongue, there occurs a very difficult situation, and one that is of particular interest because it is so extreme, because there are few guidelines for the teachers who are involved in it, and because of its immediate urgency. Teachers cannot possibly await the results of considered investigation. They have to arrive at decisions day by day, and indeed from one moment to the next. It is on their pressing dilemma, and the challenge it presents to linguistic and educational researchers alike, that I concentrate in the following chapter.

3
Multilingual classrooms

The way education is organised in this country, and many widely shared assumptions about it, support the notion of the monolingual classroom as the norm. Statistically this is of course the case. No more than a small fraction of the child population comes to school at age 5 having learned a mother tongue other than English. Those who do are concentrated in a small number of neighbourhoods, and there the concentration is such that for them and for their teachers the overall statement, expressed in terms of percentages, has no meaning at all. The interaction that is the central fact of their early educational experience is entirely determined by there being no common language. This circumstance is inescapably dominant.

Assumptions about norms in education are extremely resistant to change — and not only in this country. H.H. Stern, writing in a foreword to a collection of papers about the Canadian experience of French/English bilingualism (ed Swain, 1972) makes succinctly the point about the relationship between norms relating to language and the political context of their development: 'present day systems are still largely based on a unilingual principle which was accepted in the nineteenth century and which reflects the development of homogeneous nation states' (p. 1). Where monolingual classes are the norm, the presence of children who must become bilingual, or who are at some stage of becoming so, becomes a problem, one that is likely to be ignored when once their control of English approximates to that of other children in their age group. This is the assumption made by the considerable number of books and other publications of the late 1950s and early 1960s designed to assist teachers and others for whom the presence of children in English classrooms who neither spoke nor understood English constituted a dauntingly unfamiliar problem. Nothing in the professional preparation of many teachers had equipped them for foreign language teaching. There was a clear need and a warm welcome for books that, in general, drew upon traditions of teaching English as a foreign language, developed in relation to an international market, and were indebted too to methodologies of foreign language teaching, with an overwhelming emphasis on French, developed in this country. Many of these are still in use. The most developed and ambitious work of the 1960s was the Teachers' Book and associated teaching materials, having *SCOPE* as its general title (*Schools Council Project in English*), designed at Leeds under June Derrick's general direction. It embodies the best and most up-to-date ideas current at the time of its publication – 1967. It is still widely used, and in its recent (1979) second edition it is the presentation and the cost, rather than principles and design, that are modified. The initial publication is extraordinarily complete. Everything the teacher needs is there in the bulky wooden container called the 'Teacher's Package'. The Teacher's Book sets out in step-by-step detail two terms of lessons, in the course of which the teacher presents, and revises, a selection of English structures and vocabulary. The assumption is that there is an almost complete discontinuity between the teacher's experience hitherto, with English-speaking children, and his current work, undertaken from necessity not choice, with immigrants. For the children, the concentration on learning English language is almost complete. It is almost reluctantly acknowledged that they cannot study English all the time, and a variety of games and songs and other activities are included that provide some element of language practice. There is no suggestion relating to the maintenance or development of their mother tongue, no suggestion that being bilingual may constitute a different sort of experience from being monolingual, and in the absence of any such reference it is difficult to escape the inference that the mother tongue is to be discarded, as of no educational account. The sequel, *SCOPE 2*, is in interesting ways more innovatory. It consists of material designed to support topics, and it assumes a classroom in which everyone works in English, but controls the language in significantly different degrees, and because it also assumes that something like this (though with a lesser degree of contrast) is already familiar to the teacher, it is much less complete, substantial and developed, and judging from my observation, it has been very much less influential.

Newcomers to schooling, younger than the age for which *SCOPE* was designed, were almost (not quite) ignored. The assumption was that very young Asian children – and indeed young children generally – acquire language rapidly and readily. It was a belief that had powerful support from what was then – in the early and mid-1960s – the currently advanced and developing theoretical work on the acquisition of language (cf. ch. 1, this volume). These younger pupils had in any case a long, formative decade of the educational process ahead, and every incentive to learn from English classmates the limited English a 5-year-old is expected to control. Theoretical considerations and common-sense observation alike could be held to justify the expenditure of limited resources on older children, within a few years of being required to compete for educational and occupational opportunities with native speakers of English. There was in addition a tacit assumption that the problem, though undoubtedly acute, was temporary. A generation born in England would make its way through an English educational system untroubled by it. The number of individuals in any school not fully in control of English would diminish to a point where occasional individual assistance would be enough.

This was a view that simply took no account of the tenacity with which speech communities retain their habits, their beliefs, and the language that uniquely expresses them. Nor did it take account of the very slight motivation Asian women have for learning English beyond the level where it serves for everyday use in a very limited range of situations. Asian languages remain the normal speech of many homes and the mother tongue of children born in them. When they reach the age of 5, they are legally obliged to come to school, where the condition of their education is that they become fully interacting pupils not in the languages they have already acquired, but in a new one. Where mothers go to work, English-speaking nursery education starts earlier than 5. In some neighbourhoods, and in some schools, these children constitute a majority in any one age-group. The native speakers of English among the pupils are so few in number that they can offer neither a model of the English of young children nor an incentive to acquire it. Theirs is an extreme situation, significantly different from that of an earlier generation of immigrant children, one that affects a small minority (in terms of the population at large) but affects their education, and indeed their future, in a radical way. For closely comparable situations and for what might be learned from them, one must look outside the United Kingdom. By observing and working, as I did, with small numbers of these children and their teachers, one cannot obtain the quality or range of data that makes confident generalisation feasible, but one does observe, and in some measure experience, the confusion of linguistic experience and the formidable pressures that such situations exert on teachers and pupils alike.

The case for early schooling in the mother tongue

Concern for pupils who cannot receive their early education in their mother tongue because their teachers have no fluency in it may be a recent phenomenon in the United Kingdom, but is of long standing elsewhere. It was the subject of an international conference, and of papers published subsequently, as long ago as 1928. The case was made by a UNESCO working party in 1953 that the first stages of the educational process should be in the mother tongue, and that educational decision-makers have a clear obligation to ensure that this is practicable. The case was made on social, psychological, and linguistic grounds. Early education in the mother tongue exploits the oral fluency already gained in the interests of literacy, recognises the value of the child's individuality, helps to establish an expectation of success. None of this is easily contested. Until recently however it seemed applicable to remote and underdeveloped parts of the world, where the sparseness of elementary school provision may mean that speakers of many languages, not necessarily. intelligible to one another, may have access only to teachers who speak none of their languages and can scarcely be expected to master, at best, more than one or two of them. This is almost exactly the situation in some urban schools in the United Kingdom in the 1980s. Of these, some have a teacher, or an ancillary, who is effectively bilingual. Those that do not illustrate in an extreme degree a range of language problems that in a more diffused and less acute form, are widespread. For the newcomer to school, the unique set of meanings that he has learned with his mother tongue has no recognised place in the classroom. For society the multilingual classroom in the charge of an effectively monolingual teacher constitutes a severe problem in terms of resources and their organisation and distribution, one that Uriel Weinreich (1974) sees as independent of any attempt at social or political repression, and as just not susceptible of solutions that do not in their operation create further difficult problems:

In many areas of the world . . . it is . . . inevitable, even where there is no intention of imposing the state language upon an minority, that some children receive their instruction in a language other than their mother tongue. Not only does this retard the children's education, but their knowledge of their own language suffers, and its cultivation is neglected. (Weinreich, 1974, p. 121)

This view is supported by another distinguished sociolinguist, Bernard Spolsky, who, introducing a collection of papers on bilingual education (Spolsky and Cooper, 1977), puts the matter even more directly:

> It must be obvious to all that incomprehensible education is immoral: there can be no justification for assuming that children will pick up a school language on their own, and no justification for not developing some programme that will make it possible for children to learn the standard language and for them to be educated all the time that this is going on. Similarly, very clear arguments can be made for the value of teaching children to read in the language they speak, rather than attempting to teach a new language and initial reading at the same time. (p. 20)

It is, he adds, difficult to challenge claims like this — and as difficult to find empirical studies that unequivocally support them. It is not that there is a shortage of empirical studies of bilingual education nor of the many variations of which it is susceptible nor of a representative number of different speech communities in which it occurs. Cohen (1975) has a brief and selective review of these which is enough to demonstrate that this is so, and, in addition, shows that no consensus of views emerges about the short- or the long-term effect of bilingual schooling. It is not in these circumstances, as he points out, reasonable to expect the sort of informed agreement that could serve as a guideline for speech communities like our own, where young pupils arriving at school speaking mother tongues unknown to their teachers constitute a relatively novel and a rather local phenomenon. He does, however, identify some of the dimensions of difference among speech communities that might be expected to determine whether education in a language not native to them will, in the most general terms, accelerate or retard school learning by pupils. The size of the speech communities concerned is one of these. In addition, educational systems differ in relation to the quality and content of what they are able to offer. Languages differ in the degree of prestige they enjoy in the same society. All these and other factors bear in on the situation of the ordinary child, rising 5, who is obliged to attend daily a school where he does not readily understand his teacher, is not understood by her, where the start of literacy and everything that literacy makes accessible has to await the learning of another language, and where there are few or no opportunities for the rapid and various extension of the mother tongue that is usual in the first years of schooling. Literacy in the mother tongue, for the children in this position, is acquired, if it is acquired at all, outside the educational system, in classes set up by members of the ethnic minority of which he is a member, as a rule controlled and partially financed by the religious community. So far as institutionalised daytime schooling is concerned, the mother tongue scarcely counts. Literacy in English, fluency and confidence in spoken interaction in English, are bound to be delayed for all these children, and long delayed for slower learners among them. The bilingual fluency they eventually attain, for all its obvious practical usefulness, receives little or no recognition in the classroom.

The options available to schools and to the LEAs that control them are not numerous, and are further narrowed in a period of general, and increasingly severe, economic constraint. This in itself constitutes an effective pressure to do very little, since the teachers and children concerned constitute a minority and there is a powerful argument for concentrating on majority needs the limited resources that are available. One option is urged by the authors of the Bullock Report (1975); the extension to newcomers to schooling the withdrawal classes, taught by specialist teachers that were at the time of publication well established in relation to primary and secondary schools. Since (it is implied) these children have no alternative to receiving their formal schooling through the medium of English, the sooner they start, and the better the conditions of their learning, the less they stand to lose. One option — and an attractive one — is the employment of bilingual teachers, speakers of English and at least one widely used Asian language. There are, in addition, possible supportive strategies, of which the provision of special courses of study for teachers and future teachers, and of classes for Asian mothers, designed to increase their control of English to a point where they can confidently assist their own young children, are two. None of these options has been disregarded, and none has been vigorously pursued and sustained by a sufficiency of funding. There are real and intractable difficulties in the way of each. While the number of schools and classes involved is no more than a small percentage of the total number, it stills exceeds the number of suitably qualified and experienced people who can be appointed to posts. Bilingual infant teachers are rare, so there is a strong tendency for their energies and time to be spread over several classes. Very few native speakers of English have attained any degree of fluency in the language of Asian pupils. The methodology of foreign language teaching has traditionally had a low priority in most institutions in which primary teachers are trained. Courses of study designed to assist pre-service teachers and

Multilingual classrooms

those already in service in the dauntingly new task are, with few and recent exceptions, short in duration and broadly inclusive. They give priority to developing in teachers an understanding of unfamiliar traditions, to fostering sympathetic attitudes, to introducing well-established methods of language teaching, and to familiarising teachers with some of the materials available for their use. A range of accessible inexpensive publications having a broadly similar function became available between the mid-1960s and the mid-1970s (Derrick, 1966 and 1977; Hill, 1976; McNeal and Rogers, 1971).

Nothing in my observation suggests lack of concern for these children, either on the part of the schools or of the Local Authorities responsible for those schools. There is however a severe problem, an overall shortage of resources, in a general climate of recession. Against that background a very different approach is beginning to be influential. It is clearly apparent in the survey of language diversity in London schools undertaken by Harold Rosen and his associates (Rosen and Burgess, 1980) and in the series of films with accompanying handbook prepared by the BBC Continuing Education Department under the general title *Case Studies in Multi-Cultural Education* (Twitchin and Demuth, 1981), and in the work of the Linguistic Minorities Project. This approach involves acceptance of the multicultural and multi-ethnic character of contemporary British society as a fact affecting all its institutions, including of course its schools. It rejects the notion of multilingualism in schools as a local and temporary problem or indeed as *in itself* a problem at all, and with that notion another, nearly related, but more rarely verbalised – the idea that to be a native speaker of another language than English is to experience a condition of inherent disadvantage. This approach is established, has the support of NAME (National Association for Multi-Racial Education) and is supportive of the stance taken up by the recently established NCMTT (National Council for Mother-Tongue Teaching). It is gathering momentum. There are many schools where its effects have still to be felt.

What follows in the rest of this chapter is in effect a case study of classrooms in which the problems were experienced as constant and acute. The provision was, in a context of overall scarcity, generous, but children and teachers alike were obliged to depend very heavily on the resources they could command simply as language users. The teachers, required by the nature of their role to assume responsibility and to take initiatives exploited to the limit the experience common to all adult language-users, that of interacting with uncomprehending, or partially comprehending, listeners. Circumstances like these are not widely representative, but they are very far from unique. What happens seems to me very interesting, probably instructive, and certainly deserving of close attention.

Multilingual classroom and monolingual teachers: a case study

The school in question is newly built, well equipped. Neither in these respects nor in respect of the enthusiastic commitment of its teaching staff does it conform to the stereotype of the inner-urban primary school. It has for long had a diminishing minority of pupils for whom English is the first language. At the time when I worked there, four such children were in the reception class; in the nursery, among the thirty children who would enter formal schooling in the following term, only two. This was not the result of the currently widespread problem of falling rolls. The total number on roll was, contrary to the current trend, steadily increasing, but the increase was that of a shifting population. Newcomers to the neighbourhood were currently young Asians with growing families. The children bring to school the language of their mothers, who are speakers of one or more among several Asian languages. These young, and much-occupied women have little need for English. Of course unusually ambitious families foresee the future advantage to children of growing up bilingual from babyhood and make the very considerable effort that is needed to bring this about. For the most part English is rarely heard inside the home and even more rarely used in talk between parents and children. Husbands are expected to conduct any business the family may have with English-speaking officials. The need for literacy in English is no more than occasional. Social relationships among neighbours and relatives, everyday shopping, entertainment, the life of the religious community, are all conducted in Asian languages, and for many women the use of English is, as one would expect in these circumstances, hesitant, limited, and rare.

At school that diminishing minority of children who are native speakers of English usually play together. Punjabi chatter and laughter dominate the playground. Not that there is any sense of exclusion. My attention was drawn to one very small Asian child who had made herself the friend and protector of an even smaller English one, and who could be seen at playtime helping her to find her coat and button her shoes. It was a virtually wordless friendship. There was neither need nor incentive for the Asian children to learn English in order to secure friends and playmates. In circumstances like these, teachers, and, at a later stage, English books and teaching materials, constitute the sole English language learning resource available to children, and the expectation that they learn the sole pressing reason for acquiring English.

Of the options discussed earlier, some have already been made available. Teachers have a part-time colleague whose native language is a dialect of Gujerati, who has a good knowledge of several other Asian languages and a near-native control of English, and his ability to interpret and advise is valued and used. That he is available, and free to develop a consultant role is itself evidence of Local Authority concern and evidence of a will to allocate to schools like this generous resources, even in stringent times. In addition there is a home-school liaison teacher, on whom are focused the efforts generally made to explain to parents the reasons for the requirements the school makes and the purpose of what children do. Withdrawal groups, staffed by specialised peripatetic teachers, are available to all the children, from the first year of compulsory schooling. By any reasonable standards the provision represents a full recognition of the actual difficulties confronted by children and teachers. The difficulties persist and are severe in the face of a sympathetic environment; this constitutes their seriousness, and, of course their compelling interest.

The teachers' perspective

The teachers were emphatic that learning to speak and to understand English had priority over all else. There was no hint of complacency — on the contrary, the teachers individually and as a team were constantly on the alert for new ideas and materials that might improve their rate of success. In all their discussions there was a strong sense of the pressure of time. These children had to understand and respond in the new language, and to become literate in it. They had to do so quickly, for the price of delay was unacceptably high. Slower learners would fall behind with a curriculum which, though it took account in a variety of ways of a multi-ethnic and multilingual school population, had not shifted, and could not shift, from the premise of native fluency in English. Those who had not, by age 11, attained a near-native oral control of English, and literacy not noticeably below the standard expected of a native speaker at the same age, would find themselves a disadvantaged minority in the comprehensive secondary school, with its much larger catchment area. Of that minority, many would emerge underqualified in relation to their intelligence, disadvantaged in terms of employment prospects and in terms of extended education. There was good reason for the prevailing high level of anxiety. Some of the children did learn very fast, attaining by the time they were 7 or 8 a high level of oral fluency and a good start in literacy in English. Most needed longer, and some required more time than the primary stage offered.

My particular interest was in observing the earliest stages of the process, and especially in the spoken interaction between English-speaking teachers and their Asian pupils in the nursery and reception classes. The nursery was for a variety of reasons, economic as well as educational, highly valued by the Asian community and very well attended. Despite its legally optional character, it constituted the initial year of schooling for most pupils. I have emphasised the degree of support made available in the school. For each individual teacher, recourse to various sources of information and suggestions could be no more than occasional. Most of the time they confronted intractable problems, linguistic and educational, on their own, assuming responsibility for young children with whom they had no shared language, dependent upon their internalised knowledge and accumulated experience.

Varieties of interaction between teachers and pupils in the absence of a shared language

For these teachers of Punjabi- or Kashmiri-speaking newcomers, the many-to-one relationship of the classroom created difficulties so different in degree from those experienced by teachers of English-speaking children in the same age group as to be effectively different in kind. To get the children to understand, for example, that they must remain in one room, that they must attend to their teacher, disregarding other speakers if necessary, that they must choose one of the activities offered and continue with it for a reasonable length of time — all these constituted for them preoccupations of a very demanding kind. It seemed to them essential that their nursery classroom should approximate to accepted norms, and they worked to attain a reasonable conformity with the expectations that are embodied in classroom routines. Their priority in teaching had to be getting the children to recognise the meaning of teachers' instructions and organisational arrangements, their *directives*, to use Sinclair and Coulthard's term. The paramount requirement of safety and good order entailed a choice of emphasis on the functions, rather than on the structures of English.

Their directives were regularly brief and uncomplicated, and if to other teachers and English-speaking observers they sounded for that reason a little brusque, that impression was countered by the warmth expressed in other ways than verbally towards the children, and by the high degree of tolerance, occasionally ironic, of the delays and frustrations that frequently occurred. The teachers recognised that it was helpful to their learners if directives were expressed in the same way on each of the many occasions on which they were used. Practised and fluent native speakers have a good deal of difficulty in avoiding variation and paraphrase; to do so requires a degree of concentration not easily attained in a classroom that offered so many other urgent preoccupations. These teachers were obliged to rely more heavily than most on non-verbal communication, on showing and doing, miming and gesture. Their intonation was simple and emphatic. They constantly demonstrated what was required, accompanying the demonstration by English talk, often addressed to no more than one or two children at a time. What they provided approximated to the sort of exposure to their mother tongue that they had experienced in babyhood. The teachers worked very hard, scarcely allowing themselves a moment's respite. Whenever there was not an immediate demand on her attention one of them would deliberately initiate and sustain talk in English, remaining alert to notice and use any gesture towards communication made by a child. In the following transcript of a few moments of such interaction, one of the children glanced up from a cutting and pasting activity towards a picture of a dog. The teacher responded at once with:

Oh, it's a big doggie, isn't it? I think he must be going for a walk.
Do you like doggies?

She recognised that the child meant *something*; in this, and in her response, she does what adults usually do in responding to much younger children at an early stage of acquiring English — even to using the nursery diminutive. She seems hardly to expect replies to her questions, but rather to intend expanding the supposed utterance, making an opportunity for language use. There was however no immediate response, so she tried again, and then again:

Have you got a dog at home?
Have you?

There was a murmur, no more than an indication of attention, too faint for my tape recorder to pick up. The teacher heard it as if it had something to do with a cupboard:

It's in the cupboard? Oh, I didn't know you kept doggies in the cupboard! D'you keep him in the cupboard?

On the face of it, what is said here is decidedly strange, as adult utterances to young children often are in the hearing of other adults. There seems to be a ground rule for this sort of interaction, however, that can be verbalised easily enough where there is occasion to do so, and which these teachers regularly operated; that even where children's utterances are so hesitant as to be nearly inaudible, they are interpretable, though, since they are so young, their meanings may be quite different from those that would occur to an older child or an adult. What matters is adult attention and response. The opportunity for interactive talk has to be sustained.

On this occasion, the adult's attention to one speaker encouraged two others in succession to offer just such elliptical utterances as native English speakers, younger than these by about two years, might be expected to produce. 'Got cat' was the first utterance, then, from another speaker, 'Seen doggie' and then a rather more confident repetition of 'Got cat' from the first. These responses are not distinguishable from the data which, in the 1960s, was categorised using the terms 'pivot' and 'open' classes, and descriptively labelled 'telegraphic speech'. Cazden (1972) comments on the suitability of the label, and on the psychological immaturity in the speaker that was held to account for the brevity and incompleteness of the utterance.

Telegraphic is an accurate characterisation of a product – an utterance like 'Mommy sock' which is constructed at a particular stage of development before function words have been acquired, and while the child's programming span is still severely limited. (p. 78)

Presumably the explanation in terms of a general limitation on programming span could not be supposed to apply to these children. There seems evidence rather that the elliptical utterances belong to an early stage of language learning rather than to an early stage of intellectual development.

This teacher did not correct children's incomplete utterances or require the rehearsal of them in amended form. She ignored the ellipsis, picked up the meaning as she understood it, and tried to secure additional contributions from the children. 'A nice cat,' she agreed, and then added, pausing briefly for opportunity of reply after each question:

> What colour is it, your cat?
> What colour is your cat?
> I like black ones, 'cos they're lucky! No?
> What colour is it?

There was a response to the last question that seemed to relate to the word 'colour', likely to have been familiar to some of the children from its frequency of repetition in a variety of contexts:

> Red.

There was nothing to be made of that answer. The teacher accepted it, avoiding in discourse that was, in this as in other ways, very uncharacteristic of the classroom, any suggestion that it was inappropriate or unsatisfactory.

> A red one. Oh well.

In the passages of verbal interaction that occurred during the day these and similar features recurred. I observed one teacher who had a good deal of trouble persuading two boys to sit down and drink their milk. Nine repetitions, in all, were required. At no stage did the teacher show any impatience. She treated the matter as a simple failure of comprehension, resorted to mime, pushed one of the two into a sitting position wedged between two already seated children, and pointed him to the other as a model to be imitated. Once the two were seated, she made her satisfaction evident to them, using, as she habitually did, the deliberately exaggerated intonation pattern noticed by Snow (1972) and by Vorster (1975) as a feature of the variety adults spontaneously and habitually employ in interacting with much younger children than these.

These teachers kept to themselves their well-founded suspicion that these children were as likely as any other 4-year-olds to be deliberately disobedient. Their teaching strategy assumed a constant goodwill in the children. Failure to comply with requirements was attributed to incomprehension or to misunderstanding. It was the responsibility of adults, and specifically of teachers, to resolve mistakes. Where they could interpret a meaning intended by a child they responded to it, expanding it where possible, encouraging virtually any spontaneous contribution, avoiding the sort of response likely to be perceived as a rebuff. They were no more dismayed than are the mothers of very young children at the ungrammatical character of children's utterances, and they did not hesitate to use forms of English that, if they were initiated as a model, would have to be almost at once discarded. Their own utterances were short, very direct, and usually related to the immediate environment. They used every possibility of touch and gesture and facial expression to supplement the limitations of language. Whether or not consciously, mother-tongue teaching was their model, their own experience of rearing young families was a primary resource, their unspoken assumption was that these 4-year-olds were in a situation where they needed to learn, from teachers as surrogate parents, a second mother tongue.

There were of course obvious differences between the model and the reality. These were normally intelligent children whose acquisition of their various mother tongues was already well advanced. It was necessary only to listen to them as they played in a small room equipped with domestic furnishings to recognise that they were in confident and noisy control of a wide range of linguistic functions. There were other differences. Mothers typically interact with only one child of language-acquiring age at any one time. Even where teachers are at great pains, as these teachers were, to use every opportunity of individual attention, their priority has to be the watchful control of a large number. Untroubled concentration upon one child or on a small number is rarer than it seems. Children are exposed to the mother tongue they acquire for a great part of their waking time, whereas the school day is short, includes frequent breaks, and children are exposed to a share of their teachers' attention for no more than a few hours daily, with long intervals during school holidays. There is hardly need to invoke the possibility that for them, the critical period of language acquisition may be already on the wane, the language acquisition device no longer at its most effective, in order to explain how it is that progress towards control of English is slower and less assured than is the acquisition of the mother tongue. There is little opportunity for its use in interaction with other children of their own age. The function of English is for them for interaction with teachers, in classrooms. It is language for learning in school. They can hardly be expected to share the sense of its urgency, its critical importance for the future, which informs everything done by the adults responsible for their educational experience.

English in withdrawal classes

What is done includes the provision, once the children enter compulsory schooling at age 5, of withdrawal groups taught by specialist members of a peripatetic team to groups numbering six to eight children. From the point of view of the Local Education Authority and the school this provision represents a generous response to acknowledged need. From the point of view of pupils what is entailed is that learning English is a preoccupation of every lesson, but that there is especial concentration on English for up to half an hour on three of five working days in the week from reception class and beyond the first and into the junior school. Small numbers in withdrawal groups make possible concentrated oral practice. Individual difficulties can be identified and resolved.

The pattern of spoken interaction between pupil and teacher is typically different from that already discussed, and reflects a different set of assumptions about language learning and teaching. Both can be illustrated by quite brief quotations from the text that teacher and pupils produced. The specialist teacher assembled her group, identified each of them by name, and showed them a card having on it a coloured drawing, saying at the same time very distinctly,

This is an orange.

It was, by the time I had opportunity to observe it, a routine beginning, made familiar by many repetitions, and intended as a reassuring start. She repeated what she had said. In form it was a statement, but it was intended to be interpreted as an instruction. 'Listen and repeat after me' is the unspoken requirement that the pupil has to understand and comply with in order to earn approval. There was hesitation at the start, and several repetitions; the choral response, when it came, was hesitant. After a few minutes the teacher began a round of questions, each relating to an illustration on a card, and addressed to each member of the group in turn.

Teacher: What's this . . . what's this?
Pupil: cat . . . cat

This was not enough. A complete utterance was required, on the model offered by the teacher.

Teacher: No Ranee. 'This is a cat'.
Pupil: This is a cat.
Teacher: Good girl.

A variety of sentence patterns was then introduced and practised: 'Is it a dog? Yes it is/No it isn't.' 'What is he/she doing? He's sitting/she's standing.' Children practised questions as well as answers in what was a rehearsal of learned responses rather than spontaneous language use. This is of course very usual, orthodox, language teaching. The experience of the teacher was very apparent in the variety she introduced, in the supply of materials she had to support what she did, in the rapidity with which she noticed and praised expected answers. All the recommended conditions of success were present — the specialised assistance by an experienced teacher, the small classes, the intensive (if by intensive is meant concentrated and repetitive) teaching. These conditions derive from a methodology of foreign language learning and teaching developed in situations where opportunities for the learner to use the language, and pressures upon him to do so, are alike very restricted. Nobody, neither class teacher nor specialist, was very happy with the effects of such orthodox methods, capably employed. The gap between repetitive practice, designed to ensure the learning of sentence patterns and to improve English pronunciation and the English needed by children in school was simply too wide. There was an uneasy convergence on this question: what if established methods of foreign language teaching relate very little to the sort of learning in which children as young as these spontaneously engage? What if the use of opportunities for intensive, concentrated practice requires from the learner a degree of understanding of his teacher's purposes, and of identification with them, that is not possible for 5- and 6-year-olds? A very considerable degree of identification of purpose seems to be implied by statements intended to function as specific instructions. If the children were simply too young to recognise, in any degree at all, the purpose of repeating stretches of language, the activity must seem to them quite unrelated to that of understanding meanings and being understood. Misgivings gave rise to experiment with alternatives; all the teachers, including the peripatetic specialists, were at liberty to depart from orthodox, recommended approaches.

I had opportunity to observe a teacher arrive to teach her succession of withdrawal groups equipped with everything she needed to furnish a succession of tea parties. When the children arrived, they found the chairs placed round a table which was covered with a lace-edged cloth.

The kettle was on. As they came in and sat down they were involved in an event that required a good deal of English language production, much of it as repetitive as that of more orthodox language lessons. The teacher, in her role of attentive hostess, asked the same questions of each guest in turn. In other respects the interaction was dissimilar from that I had observed on earlier occasions. There was, for example, no requirement that complete sentences should be produced where a native speaker might very well not do so. Elliptical answers were readily accepted. Partially expressed meanings were expanded. At the same time the discourse was not that of adult and child in a domestic setting. The nearest analogy is the closest to fact — it is of an adult deliberately engaging, with children, in a make-believe. The teacher, pretending to be hostess at an English tea party, had ensured that she would be in effective control. The children were pretending to be well-behaved English guests; speaking English was a necessary part of the pretence. The teacher found opportunity, as adults commonly do in play with children, to include information about how things work. This was done effortlessly, almost casually:

Teacher: We switch the kettle on . . . see . . . now this is a special kettle.
    When it's boiled, it's going to switch off . . . see . . . you tell me
    when it's ready. Here you are . . . .

At this point each child was offered a cup, took it, and said 'thank you'. The teacher enquired next who wanted sugar.

Pupil: I like sugar!
Teacher: What do we need . . . what do we want for sugar?
Pupil: Tea!
Teacher: How do we put the sugar in the tea?
Pupil: Spoon!
Teacher: Do you want a spoon?
Pupil: I want sugar in my tea!
Teacher: Do you? You forgot to tell me.

As she spoke, the teacher kept a watchful eye on the kettle. The steam-operated switch turned off the current as soon as the water boiled.

Teacher: What has happened?
Pupil: Finished.
Teacher: It's finished.

The English taught and practised in this withdrawal group had some features of acquisition in a domestic setting, some features of the class-room. All the language related to immediate and actual circumstances and events, and the context offered the learner many clues to meaning. That context had not however occurred spontaneously. It had been contrived, at considerable cost in time spent in preparation, by the teacher, for the learning possibilities she perceived in it. She insisted, just as parents do, on routines, of 'please' and 'thank you', and, again like a parent, she seemed more concerned that what the children said should accord with the facts of adult perception than that it should be grammatically well formed. Almost any contribution made by the children received attention and a welcome, and they were encouraged to venture English that she had made available rather than items she specifically required. She included questions addressed to each child in turn, but was ready to accept minimal or hesitant replies and expand them. It seemed to me that her make-believe tea party allowed of a compromise that was a useful innovation for children at this stage, too young to comprehend what is meant by study, yet placed in a situation where the need to learn quickly was more constant and pressing than that of learners for whom most materials and methods were originally intended.

Teachers like these, working in schools where the presence of a young Asian language-speaking population presents, simply by its numbers, a severe challenge, feel with some justice that outside their own school, and neighbourhood and authority, in society at large, there is little recognition of how serious, or how intractable, their problems are. Relative to the English-speaking community, the Asian language-speaking population is quite small, and is for the most part concentrated in neighbourhoods where other problems demand even more urgent attention. Materials for the use of teachers of the younger children are designed to meet general rather than specific needs. Teachers are, even in schools that enjoy a generous range of support services, challenged all the time to use their own resources and sense that the extent to which they are required to be inventive, imaginative, and innovatory is little recognised. The situation of the child who must be educated in a language not his mother tongue is extremely demanding. Recognition of what it is to be bilingual, of the difficulty of attainment and the potential usefulness of bilingualism is still very slight. At present the development of literacy in the mother tongue is dependent on provision made outside the system of compulsory formal schooling. These are problems deserving of more widespread public attention than they currently receive.

In what follows I turn to the consideration of classrooms in which the majority of children speak the language in which they will be taught, and supply the minority for whom English is not the mother tongue with an incentive and a means of learning.

4

Language in the first school day

There are of course differences of organisation and timetable, staffing and provision among first schools, and between classes for newcomers to the educational system. For all that, the requirements of this age group, as in our society they are perceived and interpreted, are such that the observer is forcibly struck by the similarities that obtain, and familiarity in this case confirms the initial impression. There are well-established habits and expectations to which teachers, even in the exceptional circumstances of those discussed in the preceding chapter, feel obliged to conform.

The similarities immediately apparent are matters of outward appearance — the small scale of the furnishings, the brightly painted surfaces, the arrangement of the room in areas equipped for different activities, the easily accessible toys, selected for more than their amusement value. That likeness among schools extends to the distribution and organisation of time. The school day, short by adult standards, is divided into periods of intentionally contrasted activities, none of them so long as to tax children's attention span unreasonably. 'Lessons' as these are understood at later stages, where a class attends to the same topic for a length of time determined in advance and marked by bells, occupy a different, initially rather small, but increasing proportion of the time available. Because the children are so young, time has to be assigned to practical matters, like changing clothing and shoes, that will later be regarded as the children's own responsibility, requiring minimal adult supervision. In the first school, supervision, while it is often by design unobtrusive, has to be virtually continuous. Routines are established in relation to arrival and departure and the noting of absences, and additional routines are associated with the collection of small sums of money, and the distribution of milk and snacks. There are regular periods of supervised play, and sessions where children have a choice from among a number of different activities for which provision is

made. Among the available activities are some clearly recognisable to
the adult observer as brief lessons in reading or in number work, in
singing or in physical education. It is common to find much emphasis
placed, and much time spent, upon putting away the materials and
equipment after use. 'Tidying up' is often a very lengthy matter, relative to the time available for using the items that have to be put away,
and the habits of orderliness supposedly instilled are defended by
teachers as having an educational value in their own right.

Given the shortness of the available time, and the demands made on
it by organisational routines of one kind and another, often very slowly
completed where children are unused to them, there is pressure felt by
teachers to exploit the educational potential of routines, and a principal
way of doing this is, where at all possible, to engage in talk. The classroom for the youngest children allows of more variety of conversational
interaction than is common at later stages. Classroom discourse of the
sort most usual between teachers and their older pupils, where the
teacher is engaged in transmitting information, giving instructions, and
ensuring that the information is assimilated and the instructions carried
out, does occur (or at least a recognisable approximation to it occurs)
but the reception classroom is, in addition, the setting for many varieties
of talk. Talking between pupils for example, proscribed in general
between older children except where the teacher has intentionally
organised group learning, is allowed, and indeed encouraged, most of
the time. Newcomers have to learn when they may talk to each other
and when (for reasons that are hardly likely to be apparent to them)
this is not allowed. Routines have particular, and sometimes highly
specific, uses of language associated with them. Teachers who are
looking after children as they play, or as they carry out instructions, or
engage in painting and modelling and the 'creative activities' that
feature very prominently in the reception class day, talk to individuals
or small groups, very much as adults do in other settings. In addition,
there are times of the day when talking and listening are not incidental,
but are the focus of attention deliberately arranged. Teachers assemble
groups for telling or reading stories, and initiate talk, either by bringing
a topic to the attention of the group, or by requiring children in turn
to tell their own 'news'. Teachers are sometimes pressed, as a rule by
members of a generation for whom 'talking in class' was a forbidden
activity even for the youngest pupils, to justify the volume and variety
of talk that occurs daily in the first school classroom. They usually do
so by expressing the conviction that language development is a prerequisite of learning. If the topic is pursued, they draw attention to the

unreasonableness of looking for early and successful literacy where children lack previous abundant experience of spoken language, and make reference to theoretical and empirical work as discussed in Chapter 2. Work done within the Bernstein paradigm is especially likely to be invoked in defence of the position that inadequate experience of language use is causally related to educational failure. It is common to hear teachers regret that children have little opportunity outside the classroom of taking part in conversation with an adult where what that adult says is addressed to them, and of enjoying the attention of an adult listener. In saying this, they demonstrate an awareness that for many children, perhaps for most, school makes a variety of demands, and offers some opportunities that are unfamiliar to many children. This chapter is concerned to examine what these are.

Classroom routines

These are encountered early and regularly, and children quickly come to accept and respond to them – and indeed to anticipate them and to resist change. They differ, obviously, with the circumstances of schools and the preferences of teachers. For children they seem to bulk large in importance: perhaps their unlikeness to anything that happens in a domestic setting makes them memorable. That is not to say that they are learned with anything like uniform ease. In one school I had the opportunity to observe, on successive days, a teacher familiarising children with her preferred routine of registration. She liked to 'call the register' rather than simply to notice and record the arrival of individuals, on the grounds that the requirement was one they would meet repeatedly, and what was learned justified some initial expenditure of time. Accordingly, she assembled the children and reminded them of what was to happen, and what they were to do:

Teacher: Now, are you ready to answer to your names? (murmur of assent) Yes. Good. And we only answer to our *own* names, don't we? We don't say 'yes' to anybody else's.

She was right in supposing that the difficulty lay, not in responding on cue, but in refraining from response to cues heard by everyone, but directed at another individual. In order to do that, one must have some understanding at least of the purpose of the adult, and even of what it is to be a member of a class. As she anticipated, there was, within moments, a 'yes', in response to the enquiry 'Catherine?', and it did not come from Catherine. The teacher's response was good-humoured, but it left nobody in doubt that a mistake had been made, and that it was regarded as foolish:

Teacher: Who's answering? Neil? I think I'll call you 'Catherine' for the rest of the day. Shall I now?

Routines serve adult purposes and are not experienced by children as any immediate concern of theirs. Berko-Gleason and Weintraub make this point in relation to a very different routine, not part of the experience of children living in England, but widespread in the United States. They observed young Americans in process of learning what to say when warning a friendly adult, at the time of Hallowe'en, that a trick will be played if a treat is not forthcoming. The children learned at adult insistence and needed frequent reminders. Learning was not spontaneous or effortless, although a tangible reward awaited success.

The most familiar of all school routines is deliberately taught, and learned over time. This routine is called 'bidding' by Sinclair and Coulthard (1975) and I shall adopt the term. It is easily described. A *bid* requires at least two contributions. It consists of a *cue* from the teacher, normally realised by 'Hands up'. There are of course other possibilities, 'Come on!', 'Well now!', or an enquiring and expectant look that pupils are expected to interpret. The correct responses are two: those who (rightly or not) believe they know an answer which the teacher will regard as acceptable, raise their hands. Those who do not know — they fail to understand the question, or they know no answer which they think would find acceptance — wait attentively, since this is their chance to hear it again, and to learn from doing so. The teacher then indicates by name (or sometimes by an easily recognisable substitute, 'you in the yellow jersey', 'you — one of the boys this time', 'somebody who hasn't answered yet') the willing individual who is to answer. By this *nomination*, she gives that pupil sole right to speak, and he or she can expect to do so without interruption from competitors. Further, he can expect to know immediately whether he was right in believing that his answer would be acceptable. *Evaluation* by the teacher, realised simply as 'good', 'right', 'yes' or, more elaborately, with additional *comment* on the topic, or with some qualification, realised by the intonation or sometimes verbally 'good — but there's more to it than that. . .', 'yes, but there's something else we know about it', has to follow. This feedback is essential; it is acknowledgment, with or without evaluation and comment, and distinguishes teachers' questioning of their pupils from the questions and answers that are exchanged in other contexts. The speaker who offers the answer requires it, but so do the other members of the class, especially those who offered no bid, and for whom the whole exchange constitutes a chance to learn.

Unless my observation is untypical, few teachers expect *bidding* in the initial weeks of schooling, but they do teach it within the first school year. This piece of interaction was recorded in a class of 5-year-olds during their first summer term. Some of them had started in September, and had been joined by later comers. The lesson has all the appearance of having been already rehearsed on a number of previous occasions not recorded.

Teacher: Children, what did I say? What did I say yesterday about all
    shouting out together? Can I listen (raising her voice) to everybody
    talking at once? (a murmur of expected dissent) How *many* people
    can I listen to at once?
Pupils: (breaking in in anticipation) One.
Teacher: And what happens if everybody shouts at once?
Pupils: (together) Can't hear.
Teacher: (with an unmistakable air of finality) I can't hear *anybody*.

The desirability of *bidding*, as opposed to simply answering, is presented as a matter of common agreement, an arrangement in the common interest, and this can only reflect the teacher's understanding that where there are competing claims on her attention, a procedure that allows her to select among them is a necessity. For the children it is a regulation that puts a restraint on them, and it is readily overlooked, especially where the level of interest is high. Teachers of older pupils than these expect to issue reminders, and in many classrooms, as in this one, the reminder itself develops some of the characteristics of a routine.

Although for most adults, the practice of bidding – the raised hands, the hardly controlled eagerness to be heard – remains strongly associated with the process of schooling, it is not unique to the classroom. Something recognisably like it is found wherever there are many potential speakers, each having equal right of access to one, to whom is assigned the responsibility for ensuring that the threat of confusion, always present in such a situation, is not realised. Bidding, in the circumstances of a committee meeting, for example, sometimes entails the raising of hands, but a slighter gesture than that typical of the class-room is usually reckoned appropriate. 'Catching the chairman's eye' is a frequent mode of bidding. Sometimes a variety of verbal realisations is used instead. These are as a rule consciously formal, as if designed to disclaim too much eagerness or any suggestion of self-importance in the speaker. Participants in meetings differ noticeably in the adroitness they display in securing the chairman's attention, and the answering nomination (often equally oblique in its realisation) that gives the right to hold the floor. Some people never acquire much skill in securing a turn, and not all chairmen are adept at noticing bids or indeed at recognising the extent of their responsibility for distributing talking turns among those present. The analogy between class and teacher, committee and chairman, is quite close, and suggests that the routine of bidding is a less local or more significant matter than is often sup-posed. What is readily observable in classrooms is extendable to dis-course generally. Bidding is a realisation of a strategy for the reasonable distribution of turns where groups are large, and one person in the group exercises authority, along with recognised privileges and rights. Children, still inexperienced participants in discourse, take time to come to terms with it, need and get frequent explanation, often ignore the rules once learned and sometimes patently fail to recognise its purpose or to use the strategy appropriately. It is common for instance to see a child approach a teacher whose attention he has already secured, waving a raised arm, as though this gesture were a signal required to assert his right to a hearing. He has not learned that where the talk is between two people, or is confined to a small group, other signals are enough to indicate whose turn it is to speak. Learning to be a pupil, a participant in classroom discourse, is not a single or a simple matter, and there is no reason to suppose that the different sorts of learning required occur in the same way. Classroom routines seem to adult onlookers to be easily and quickly learned. They are less so than they seem, and in the uncertain process of mastery, children have to gain some understanding of adult purposes and perceptions that they cannot be expected to share.

Talk associated with supervised play

Much time is given to play in early schooling, and teachers attach a great deal of importance to it. It is assumed that far from providing change and relaxation (as their various sorts of play are commonly supposed to do for adults) play provides children with opportunities for the exercise of concentrated attention, allows them to explore their environment and their developing power to control it, and is the means by which collaborative activity is first experienced. Generous provision for varied sorts of play constitutes the most noticeable change in the contemporary classroom environment relative to that which was usual before the Second World War. Play in the classroom allows of talk among children and between teachers and children. Its quality is regularly a concern of teachers — not, of course, their first concern. That must be the children's welfare and safety, and where that is threatened, even in the mildest degree, teachers must be alert to step in with whatever action or instruction they judge to be necessary.

Much of the time nothing like that is necessary, and a play session offers opportunities to observe and record spontaneous talk on which there are few constraints. Children who give brief and hesitant responses to teachers' questions when they are members of an assembled group, find it perfectly natural when released to play, to take initiatives and to assert their wishes and protect their rights. This excerpt from the play of several 4- and 5-year-olds was recorded in a crowded Wendy house. The occupants were sharing out the parts in the domestic drama, and preparing to act them out:

. . . going to play mummies and daddies,

one of them announced, and immediately came a rejoinder,

Can I be a baby?

followed by discussion, in which a third child joined:

I'll be a big boy and *you* be a baby.
I'll be a mummy.
I'll be a big girl.

Then play started in earnest, as the child who was taking the mother's part said,

Now in the cot . . . you two . . . you two got to go out and play. . . .

On another occasion a less easily identified game was observable, where one child made a deliberately ridiculous assertion, and another attempted to outdo it. The game began with an indication that something unusual was going to happen.

C'mon little girl! c'mon little girlie! c'mon quick!

The shape of the game soon emerged, not at first very clearly, because the environment was rather noisy. Two children were engaged at this point —

First speaker: You want a . . . (inaudible) to eat?
Second speaker: You want to eat a little rat?
First speaker: You want to eat a . . . (inaudible)?

By the time I recognised the nature of the contest, so had other listeners, and a little group gathered. What was intended was a formal exchange of insults, similar to the game of 'sounding' played (and known by various names) by black English speakers, and, as in sounding, the more unexpected, indeed outrageous, the item the better the turn. These children managed:

You want to eat a lion?
You want to eat a . . . (inaudible) dummy?
You want to eat a . . . on the floor? . . . no you can't.
You want to eat a pram?
I've got you . . . no.
You want a dinosaur to eat?

For players of the game and their audience alike language clearly had a function as the vehicle of fantasy. Language was used, in addition, to accompany make-believe. Domestic play in the Wendy house was varied by games of 'hospitals' and 'buses'. Chasing games, and variations on 'cops and robbers' suggested by current television series, succeeded these. None was sustained for long. The children could suppose a situation imitative of the world of adult experience, but were not at that age able to extend the make-believe into a succession of events. What Halliday calls the *imaginative* function of language, the function of pretending, already included the possibility of pretending that the world might be turned topsy-turvy, that sense might give way to nonsense, and that the rules we all know might dissolve. These uses of language seemed, from what I could observe, to be still quite undeveloped and the children seemed not yet able to maintain a fiction long enough to allow the emergence of a story.

Creative activities

This was the name given to the periods of time during which the children had access to the large toys and to a section of smaller-scale toys and games designed so as to give opportunity for (among other things) dexterity in manipulation and recognition of differences of shape, size and colour. In addition they were provided with varied painting and modelling materials. Making and building, colouring and sticking, were on offer, and children were allowed to move between the activities with some freedom. Teachers supervised, controlled, demonstrated and helped. There was associated talk, and in these circumstances that talk was typically highly contextualised and very elliptical, so much so as to be very often incomprehensible to someone not familiar (as all teachers of this age group are) with the sort of classroom I have described. Without knowing the circumstances of this interchange, for example, it is hard to determine *what* the participants mean, though the sense is strong that *they* know:

First speaker: Does that go in there? Does that go in there?
Second speaker: Yes. This one goes in . . . goes in . . . this one goes
    in . . . that one's gone away. . . . There *that* . . . and *that*.

In fact these two were together engaged in completing a formboard, and they were doing so quickly and successfully, since they had each (it appears from what they say and what they do) arrived at the solution to this sort of simple jigsaw. (You look for a space which corresponds in size and shape to the piece you have in hand.) Their language is extremely inexplicit, and, because it relates to immediate shared experience, it is entirely economical and effective. For the purpose of collaborative activity it could hardly be better. Teachers' language, in similar circumstances, is just as context-dependent. Examples are so frequent that they recur constantly in a substantial body of recorded text. The following (taken almost at random) will serve as illustration: a child asks the question,

    Why are you joining that together?

and the reply is

    You can move round the table next time.

Some murmuring goes on, evidently audible to the teacher, but not to the observer, and then:

Teacher: Is it? Do you know what these are?
Pupil: *She's* getting a lot.
Teacher: It's macaroni. You've got a lot of glue there, haven't you?
Pupil: What's that?
Teacher: It's a bead.

Isolated from its context, this seems almost meaningless: to those taking part the meaning is in no doubt at all. They are seated at a round table, and the teacher is sitting down with them. The business of the morning is the making of patterns in low relief by securing pasta shapes, beads, shells, and similar small objects to a coloured card surface. The objects that are accessible to any one individual depend upon where he or she is sitting – these are multi-purpose tables, and they are a little too large to be ideally suited to the sharing of a common stock of materials by those whose reach is short. Within the context of shared experience and similar perceptions – a context generally lacking in more formal lessons, where adult and young children can have only the haziest notion of the meanings present to each other's minds – the children find it easy and natural to ask questions of the teacher. Sometimes, but not always, they are heard and answered. I could find no evidence of a well-defined and describable difference between the very elliptical, entirely adequate English these 4- and 5-year-olds used among themselves, and that which their teacher, interacting with them, used in situations of this sort. The generalised contention, that a formal and explicit variety of English, an elaborated code in the sense discussed here on pp. 37-42, is used and is expected in school, a variety familiar to some children and unfamiliar, emotionally distant, and no more than partially comprehensible to the majority, simply found no support in my observation and recording. If a heavily contextualised, highly elliptical, inexplicit variety should be identified as a restricted code, then a restricted code was the usual English of the classrooms I observed in and worked in during a significant part of each day's duration. It was a language not distinguishable from that where, in a domestic or other setting, an adult looks after children, is responsible for them, shows them how to do things, and does her best to cope with their questions.

Story-telling and reading aloud

Where stories were told or read, songs taught and sung, conversation deliberately initiated and sustained, wherever in fact language use was the focus of attention, a rather different set of demands was made. These sessions occurred very regularly, and were regarded by teachers as a significant contribution to language development, and a prerequisite of successful literacy. Stories were chosen for their uncomplicated and attractive narrative, for their repetitive character, and for their lively illustrations. They were told or read to large groups. This was a class (as distinct from an individual or a group) activity. Of necessity, the prime demand made on the children was that they should listen with understanding, and the expectation was that they could do this easily enough for the experience to be a pleasurable one. Teachers were adept at it in general, displaying the illustrations without losing the momentum of the tale, distinguishing, by intonation, gesture and expression, the narrative from the conversational passages, signalling where repetition invited the listeners to participate in chorus. With all their skill, they could not retain the attention of *all* the children even to the shortest story. To listen and to understand and remember a sequence of events was evidently beyond the stage some of them had reached at entry to school. The assumption made, and not as a rule questioned, was a simple one. Time, and repeated exposure to the experience, would take care of the matter.

At intervals in the story, and at its conclusion, teachers undertook what it was usual to call 'discussion', but what would be more accurately described simply as a short lesson. Questions were asked that checked the recall of people and events in the story, and sometimes invited comment on them. In the following excerpt, the teacher has just told the story of the three little cats, and the questions she asks seem to be designed to get the children to reconstruct the story, and to add to it anything they can from what they know about real cats. What follows suggests that they have already learned that the questions asked by the teacher require brief answers. They seem not yet to recognise that answers that have to do with their own preoccupations, rather than with the facts of the story, or the facts of the world of shared experience, just will not do. There is early opportunity to learn that it is the teacher, not the pupil, who makes the crucial decision about what is, and is not relevant. In practice this may not be a decision at all easily made. It is not unusual for a teacher to be, as she is here, at a loss to interpret a child's meaning and to evaluate the contribution satisfactorily:

Teacher: The little white cat wants to keep the reel of cotton. Oh dear. Out come their claws. Can you see them?

Pupil: Yes.
Teacher: How many have they got? How many claws have they got
   Chatinder, do you think?
Pupil: 1, 2, 3.
Teacher: You think they've got 3?
Pupil: I think they've got 4! . . . 4.
Teacher: Do you?
Pupil: 'Cos I'm 4!
Teacher: Oh I see.

The teacher may very well reflect that the answer supports the Piagetian model of children's cognitive development; the child's answer does seem unequivocally egocentric. The teacher's non-committal response would be interpreted by more experienced and older pupils as negative, but not by these. For two of the others, ages and birthdays are altogether more interesting to talk about than are cats and the number of their claws, and they offer answers as if the question had been put to the group at large . . . .

   I'm 4!
   Rachel's 4 too!

At this point the teacher decides to bring their attention back unmistakably to what she has determined shall be the topic of the day, and she does it by means of an instruction, and another question.

   Look at the cats. Where do they have their claws?

These children are in the process of becoming pupils, and the text they and their teacher produce is partially well-formed, but no more than that. They know they have to give short responses to the teacher's questions, but they are not very good at guessing what sort of answers will be acceptable, nor at interpreting the indication given by the teacher of how well, or badly, they have done. Nor do they recognise yet that the right to change the topic belongs to the teacher, and to nobody else in the room. Arguably it is by means of just such exchanges as these that they learn.

   Discourse rules and social rules operate in close association. As the children learn to predict from one moment to the next and to venture contributions on the basis of that prediction, they learn too that teachers may interrupt and not be interrupted, that lessons impose constraints from which in other circumstances — when engaged in creative activities or in various sorts of play, for example, they are in great part free. The rules that govern the limits on spontaneous initiatives by children were not regularly nor easily remembered though. Teachers identified a child who talked when they were speaking for emphatic disapproval:

Neil, will you stop talking when I'm talking. Then you can
talk in a moment.

Most of the rules that operate to make classroom discourse predictable and orderly are not apparent to participants in it. This one is, and one answer at least to the question Sinclair and Coulthard (1975) pose —

How does the five year old who speaks when he wants to become
the ten year old who waits to be nominated? (p. 113) —

is that teachers insist that he does. There is, of course, more to it than that.

Early lessons in number and reading

In my observation, lessons in number and reading were taught to children seated in small groups, and the teacher (or teachers, for more than one was often available) moved among them. Those children who were not being taught either 'got on with their work' — using practice materials of various sorts — or were sometimes engaged on other sorts of activity altogether. Such arrangements required the teacher to keep detailed records in order to ensure that every pupil got a balanced programme spread over a day or two, but in return gave the advantages that go with the small group and much flexibility in deciding how long a lesson should last. When the attention of a group flagged, and could not readily be recalled, the teacher could direct them to another activity, and move to another group.

Lessons in reading and number were generally much shorter than the timetabled 'periods' marked by bells, that become so familiar a part of the children's later experience of school. Their structure, however, approximated quite closely to that of primary and secondary school lessons. They were made up of distinct sections, present to the mind of the teacher and clearly signalled to the pupils, sections that Sinclair and Coulthard call *transactions*. The start of a new transaction, a fresh topic or approach or activity, was signalled by the teacher by what they call a *boundary exchange*. What the teacher said had not, and was not meant to have, any other than an organising function. From the beginning, teachers assumed that utterances like these (all quoted from transcriptions of text recorded in reception classrooms within weeks of the beginning of the school year) would be understood.

> Right. We'll have just one more go. . . .
> Right. Let's count what we've got left in here.
> Now. Just a minute. Let me tell you what you've got to do.
> Now. When the pointer's in the middle, it means that both sides
>   weigh the same. . . .

There would follow a sequence of *teaching exchanges*, and optionally, a conclusion as deliberate as this:

> There we are! Now we've finished the piece of work that's set to do.

Within *transactions*, *exchanges* were generally well defined. The teacher made the *initiating move* as a rule; expected a response, persevered, if necessary, by repeating or paraphrasing or varying her initiative, until she got a response she could accept, then she evaluated the response, positively wherever that was possible, neutrally if (as in the example cited earlier, p. 60) the response was, in any ordinary adult interpretation, wide of any possible mark, and proceeded to the initiating move of the next exchange. The initiating moves (like the boundary exchanges) were typically brief and emphatic, the teachers were prepared to repeat their instructions and their questions to suit the different degrees of attention, and the varying speed of response accorded by their listeners. Standards of evaluation were more lenient than they would be later, and very tentative efforts got warm encouragement. Children were not, until a little later, required to bid; instead, most teachers preferred to nominate them in turn, so that each got an opportunity to contribute and to earn praise, without being obliged to compete for it. The sort of organisation I have described made all this possible. If nobody gave any response, the teacher would eventually supply one; if a 'wrong' answer were forthcoming, she would repeat the question with a more emphatic intonation, as if to suggest that the mistake might have been the effect of mishearing the question. Given that most children do very much want to please their teacher, these introductory lessons in the basic subjects provided frequent and repeated opportunity for them to learn what is expected of a pupil, and the texts record evidence of individual shift from partial to increased understanding. One lesson I observed was concerned with classifying on the basis of shape; circles have to be selected from a collection of pieces of various shape, colour, and thickness. Initially the pupil seemed not to recognise that a teacher's questions, addressed to her, require an attempt, at least, at an answer, and the teacher herself supplies the lack:

Teacher: Sarah, can you tell me anything about these? Are any of
   them circles?
Pupil: No.
Teacher: So where can we put them? (no response, so, after a pause)
   We can put them all there. Can we put them all there?
Pupil: Yes.
Teacher: Go on then.

Moments later, within the same transaction, a number of children have learned, not just the name that identifies the shape, but what you have to do when the teacher asks a question:

Teacher: What do we call this shape?

Nearly all the children want this time to fill the waiting slot, and there is a chorus of 'circle'. At a later stage, this teacher will almost certainly check the noisy response, but not yet. She recognises and seizes the moment:

Teacher: What is it Sarah?
Pupil: A circle.

There is no reason to suppose that this teacher — or her colleagues, from whose early lessons examples and quotations could just as well have been taken — verbalised what she did in the terms in which I have described it, any more than adults interacting with much younger children in ways that seem just as spontaneous and natural, are deliberately and intentionally engaged in familiarising them with the alternating structure of conversation. That part of the first school day, none the less, to which teachers accord priority, as parents do, the lessons they are most reluctant to abandon or abbreviate, where they see themselves exercising to the full the professional skill gained by training and experience, is designed to teach early and thoroughly that teachers' questions require from a learner a demonstration of what he knows or can do; that the demonstration must be brief and immediate (the others want their turn), and that when it *is* his turn, but not otherwise, the learner can expect not to be interrupted, and to have his effort rewarded. My experience of the professional pre-service education of teachers suggests that the adroitness and consistency with which teachers of young children do all this, owes little, if anything, to their initial training. No more than incidental attention is as a rule paid to the detail of verbal interaction in classrooms during this training process. The skill that is displayed owes more to the fact that teachers were, like everyone else, once school pupils, and that the rule-governed structure of the interaction between teacher and learner is a culturally trans-mitted fact, like the language itself. It holds wherever the educational process is institutionalised in a similar way, and it is so deeply inter-nalised that our difficulty is not in apprehending it, but in supposing that knowledge, information, or skill could possibly be transmitted in any other way.

A cross-cultural comparison is worth making briefly here. It is a significant one, and I shall return to it. Susan Philips (1972) describes the frustration of English-speaking American teachers at the sullen taciturnity (as it seemed to them) of their Amerindian pupils, for whom learning was essentially a private, if not a secret, activity, involving concentrated watching followed by unobserved practice. In our culture, conversely, there is an assumption that learning entails the possibility of being wrong, and being seen to be wrong. Risks must be taken. Teachers do their best to ensure that pupils are not so often mistaken, or so entirely at a loss, that their confidence in themselves or their expecta-tion of success overall is seriously threatened. They do not always succeed. A minority of children develop strategies that enable them to avoid taking risks; they learn a variety of ways of evading or diverting their teacher's attention. Within the contexts with which we are familiar, these strategies, and the conditions that encourage their development, are seen by teachers generally as they were seen by the teachers Philips studied, not as alternatives but as deviations, negative in their effect on learning.

Perceptions of the language of the first school classroom

Not all the sorts of language exchanged at various times of the school day ranked with teachers as equally important. Where the interaction was informal and unplanned, they made as much use of it as they could, talking and listening as much, and as intently, as other, more pressing, preoccupations allowed. Those occasions when 'lessons' were taught, when groups were assembled and the teacher took undisputed control, deciding when to start, how much digression was permissible, and when to draw the whole matter to a conclusion, were seen as central and significant in a way that other activities were not. During these, usually short, episodes the children's experience approximated to what would later occupy most of the day. And in one school in which my observations were made, the transition from the nursery to the reception class was marked by a shift of emphasis in the direction of 'lessons', and the teaching of reading and number began in earnest. From the child's viewpoint, lessons were different from 'creative activities' in that there were fewer choices for him to make, and he was expected to keep still for longer. In addition, there were sometimes quite explicit instructions, more often clues in what the teacher said, her intonation, gestures and expression, and from these clues he had to make, and test out, a guess. Teachers, and at least some pupils, perceive the business of listening and responding as more significant to the proper business of school than anything else that goes on during the day. Parents as a rule concur, supposing lessons to constitute real learning and, very often, other activities as representing a necessary concession to the fact that very young children cannot be expected to concentrate for more than brief periods of time. The text that children and teachers between them create during such lessons has often been informally described. Typically the teacher talks more than all the other participants. She takes the initiatives and the successful responses are those she anticipates. That she talks *more*, simply in terms of the number of words uttered, may be accidental or trivial, that she has more options and more, and different, responsibilities, certainly is not. The minimal, inescapable requirement that a child must meet if he is to function as a participating pupil is not very extensive. It is necessary to accept adult direction, to know that you say nothing at all unless the teacher indicates that you may, to know that when your turn is indicated you must use whatever clues you can find, and make the best guess you can. There are prerequisites to learning this. It is necessary to want adult attention and approval, and to be able to attend to a person or to a topic for more than a moment or two. Most 5-year-olds and many 4-year-olds can do this. Not all can. There has to be a code in common. It is the virtual absence of this prerequisite that constitutes for the teacher who does not speak the mother tongue of young newcomers so formidable a set of difficulties and obliges her to make the fullest possible use of non-verbal and non-vocal modes of communication.

Because the teacher has so much control of the discourse, and a unique degree of responsibility in relation to it, it is possible for her to go a very long way towards the production of an approximation to well-formed classroom discourse with minimal contribution from any of the children. This is the characteristic of classroom discourse that Joyce Grenfell recognised and, as an entertainer, unforgettably exploited. Given that she could depend upon her audience knowing a good deal about the way assemblies of small children behave, she was able, by her skilful impersonation of a well-intentioned teacher, enduring the sort of harassment that rules out any possibility of critical detachment, secure from her audiences a sort of collaboration in imagining the unheard responses of imagined children. In real classrooms, some participation from some children is all that is required for the production, in collaboration with the teacher, of recognisably well-formed discourse. That production is, for the teacher, the expected, reassuring indication that the lesson is going well, that the children are within control, and that educational purposes are being realised.

The structure of discourse has to do with the exercise of control, and the expression of unequal social relationships — that is not of course to say that it does not serve other purposes, or that it does not entail useful, beneficent activity. Children learn before entry to school that control is the prerogative of adults who, from a child's perspective, own the world and decide what happens in it. The way in which language is acquired at the earliest stages ensures the learning of that lesson; it is in no way surprising that children should enter school anticipating that adults will take charge, will tell them what to do, and will have expectations with which they must comply. Understanding that this is so, children make mistakes, fail to notice clues, or misinterpret them, know they have to make a guess, but guess (apparently) at random. Learning to be a pupil entails feeling secure enough to take the risk of mistakes and to recognise negative evaluation on the part of a teacher for what it is, even when it is indirectly expressed. Classroom interaction requires of participants that they apprehend something of each other's dissimilar representation of the world. Meanings are a matter of negotiation between those who take part, and the classroom is a place where processes of negotiation can be observed in discourse that is not exceptionally but normally partial, unequal, faltering and incomplete.

5

The rules of the game

So far, the talk that goes on in classrooms has been considered as essentially orderly, and the familiar analogy of a game, constituted by its rules, has been used more than once. In this chapter I want to consider more closely what is meant by 'well-ordered', predictable, and rule-governed, and to describe the model which, of those already referred to (in chapter 2 above) I find more comprehensive and more applicable to my purposes than others currently available, and to do so in more detail, and in a more systematic way than my references to it so far have allowed me to do. I shall want to give some account of the description developed by the Birmingham team and published under the title *Towards an Analysis of Discourse: the English used by Teachers and Pupils* (Sinclair and Coulthard, 1975, abbreviated from this point to *TAD*), and to make some reference to later and current developments of it. In conclusion, I shall offer some samples of text which is analysed using the coding system derived from the description.

Normative and constitutive rules

To describe classrooms as orderly, and the talk that occurs in them as rule-governed, is to invite a confusion that needs to be considered and not too briefly discussed. In any discussion relating to the educational process, 'rules' will be associated with regulations that relate to children's behaviour, including what they may say and when. These are prescriptive, or normative rules. They differ in detail between institutions, though they have a common function — that of ensuring safety, and securing minimal disturbance in circumstances where large numbers are required to assemble and remain in one place, engaged in a series of prescribed activities, for determined lengths of time. These rules, even when they are carefully framed, consistent, and reasonable, are often found irksome and are frequently infringed. Orderly classes, in the everyday sense, are those in which serious infringements are few, and readily contained, where the teacher's control is asserted without much show of authority, where pupils are no more noisy than the nature of their activity requires, and the teacher can impose his sense of what is appropriate, and secure pupils' collaboration in what he usually represents, to himself and to them, as a common endeavour. Classes are not always like that; the interests of pupils and teachers are frequently in conflict, teachers are not always successful in asserting their adult authority. Pupils may step out of line because they do not know exactly where the line is drawn, or because they know what the rule is perfectly well, and are determined to flout it. It may be quite impossible for the teacher to know whether or not a given breach of the rules is or is not deliberate. School rules are deliberately framed, are verbalised, and as a rule are put in writing, are insisted on more or less consistently, and may be changed. An expensive new floor is constructed, and a rule is instituted insisting that pupils remove their shoes before stepping on it, or, more significantly, there is a change, over time, in the way society believes that children should be brought up, and rules of long standing come to seem old-fashioned and repressive, and are abandoned. In everyday use, and especially in classroom use, the word 'rule' is understood and used in a similar way to relation to language. Teachers are well aware of one at least of the rules of English spelling (i before e except after c). They recognise that there are rules of concord ('we don't say "all of them was" ') and are aware of rules that seem less important than they once did ('you mustn't split infinitives'). Rules of this sort have to be at once qualified. The teacher who quotes the first has to add 'and in "weird" '. Not all varieties of English distinguish between the singular and the plural in the past tense or the verb to be. Some speakers, and some very distinguished writers of English, *do* split infinitives. These are rules designed to prescribe particular sorts of linguistic behaviour. M.A.K. Halliday compares them to table manners — they have a place, they are not absurd, but they are inessential, and they have as little to do with the negotiation of meanings as table manners have to do with nutrition. It is convenient (though not usual) to call rules of this sort 'prescriptions' or 'conventions' so as to distinguish them from the rules that constitute the systems (of sound or grammar of discourse) of a language. Users of language operate the rules simultaneously at all levels; they do so effortlessly, but they are aware of the existence of the rules as soon as they are breached, they can correct their own and other people's mistakes, and they are aware too of variations in the operation of the rule systems within the speech community. These are the rules that linguists are concerned to make articulate and explicit, and the task is a descriptive rather than a prescriptive. It is not concerned with the making of value judgments or the expression of preferences, a matter of making apparent the regularities that occur in actual use rather than of recommending conformity to particular sorts of linguistic behaviour. The rules of discourse of this second sort are discernible in text, though they are not apparent to those who create it, any more than those same speakers are aware of the grammatical regularity of their individual utterances. Because rules, in the sense of regularities, are not normally present to the consciousness of those who, day in, day out, create immense quantities of classroom text, they are not identified, defended, or insisted on. Like grammatical rules, they are noticeable only when they are breached, and explanation is sought and found as a rule in terms of forgetfulness, or misunderstanding, or inattention. Where participants observe the regularities, accept the constraints the situation imposes, and proceed, as it seems to them, naturally and normally, well-formed, orderly discourse is the outcome. These are not normative but constitutive regularities. Infringements of the first are assumed to be deliberate, and if they are regarded as serious, the usual response is some degree of moral censure. Breaching constitutive regularities, saying what was not predicted and is ill-formed, gets a quite different response. It is seen as odd, even bizarre, the product of mishearing or misunderstanding, and in need of explantion, but no sort of moral judgment is thought appropriate. Although participants in discourse are as a rule unaware that they are taking part in ordered activity, it is none the less possible to formulate the regularities they observe, and to show how those regularities are realised in particular texts by means of a coding system derived from the description. The process represents a considerable investment of time, and the question has to be posed, in this chapter and again at a later stage of the book, what purposes are served by such analyses?

Having contrasted two senses of 'rule', regulation and regularity, the normative and the constitutive, and made it clear that an orderly classroom differs in kind from orderly discourse, I have now to acknowledge a limitation on the description I have used. The spectrum of classroom verbal activity is, I have argued, a wide one; that part of the range which has been the subject of linguistically motivated research is rather restricted. The Birmingham team (in *TAD*) acknowledge this, pointing out that the interaction of pupils in discussion groups, for example, is not taken into account. What they offer is in fact rather more variously applicable than they claim. The system is, however, as Burton (1981) points out in an admirably clear and detailed exposition of the model and of the coding system derived from it, not designed to handle the language interaction of unruly classes. Since it would obviously be useful to teachers and others to have a principled account of the verbal interaction of pupils at the point where the teacher starts to lose control of their behaviour, it is natural to ask why not? In part the answer is historical. The interest of the Birmingham team was, and remained, an interest in the structure of discourse, and they were drawn to focus upon classroom interaction because it is normally controlled, purposeful, and (in the everyday sense) well-ordered. Further, the difficulties of recording what happens when classes do get out of control need no emphasis, and would be matched, or exceeded, by the near impossibility of transcribing the babel of sound characteristic of a class (of any age) that has rejected the control of the teacher. It is hard however to escape some sense of disappointment if the insights that can be had from using the system do not relate to the problems that require most urgent attention, or like this one, create the severest challenge to the educational system and the resourcefulness of the individual, and provoke the most severe anxiety. I believe that in fact the disclaimers are unnecessarily sweeping; that a pupil who rejects the authority of his teacher normally starts by breach of the rules of classroom discourse, that where these rules are observed, the classroom is, in the usual sense, orderly. The reverse is not the case however; that disordered discourse is created by interaction in a disorderly class is not true for example in classrooms where young learners, having incomplete knowledge of the discourse rules, are taught by someone easily and confidently in charge of an assembly that is still in process of becoming a class.

Rules of grammar and rules of discourse

The idea of rules at every level of language is a familiar one. Language is patterned activity at every level of its organisation. Until rather recently, the description of language concentrated on the sentence and the parts of which it is made up, leaving the study of those larger units which are comprised of sentences to the very different approach associated with the study of rhetoric. The study by linguists of rules that operate outside sentence boundaries, and relate to units larger than the sentence, is relatively recent. There is nothing new, though, about the recognition that there *are* such rules. Adults know, and children learn, that a spoken or a written text may be decidedly odd, and in need of amendment, even though it is, so far as vocabulary and grammar are concerned, beyond reproach. Teachers are very familiar with exercises, set for pupils at upper primary and secondary level, that require them to study sets of sentences. These may be offered as varied exemplifications of the operation of one or more rules, or they may illustrate the use of vocabulary in context, or pupils may be required to change some element in the sentence. These groups of sentences do not belong together. They are set out, and as a rule are numbered, so that the typography signals that these sentences do not cohere to make a paragraph. Pupils sometimes (not often) make the mistake of supposing that they do, and are puzzled at the nonsensical meanings that seem to emerge. Adults never confuse unrelated sentences with cohesive paragraphs; they are able to distinguish the two, even when all the typographical clues are removed (for example by reading the sentences aloud) and where the sentences of a paragraph are separated and jumbled they can usually restore the original order, or an order closely approximating to it, without difficulty. Users of English (and other languages) have an operational knowledge of cohesiveness which it is the job of linguists to describe and to explain. Adults understand, in addition, that situations constrain what can rate as coherent and well-ordered. Questions anticipate answers; this is a usual rule that may not hold in certain well-defined situations. The questions, for example, of a preacher addressed to a congregation not only do not require answers, but cannot be answered without at the same time challenging very seriously the speaker's assumption of authority. What rate as expected and ordinary forms of address in some situations, for example those of counsel towards a judge and towards each other, would, outside that specific setting and among the same participants, be reckoned deferential to the point of absurdity. Some things cannot be said in committee, even though they may be true, important, and necessary, without at the same time usurping the rights and responsibilities of the chairman. Nobody expects children to understand how situational rules operate until they have experienced a wide variety of different situations. Adults do however try to teach children what to say, and what they must expect to hear, in situations unlike those given as examples above, which are virtually confined to adult life, and which they may expect actually to encounter. They teach how to behave as a host and as a guest, what to say on giving a present or on receiving one, what to say to a very elderly or to a very ill person, for example. What is conventionally appropriate varies between cultures, not just between countries that may be geographically near neighbours, but between groups within a single speech community. Fortunately adults are as a rule tolerant of children who, faced with an unfamiliar situation, say the wrong thing, or withdraw into silence and awkwardness because they do not know what should be said.

The classroom is initially an unfamiliar situation. Rules that relate to the cohesiveness of text, to information that is shared, and information that is new, rules that are specific to the situation of the classroom have all to be learned by the newcomer as he goes along. He has no option in this, and in this respect early school experience is simply the first of many experiences where the individual confronts a new situation having established rules which he supposes (not always correctly) to be familiar to everyone else. There are obvious reasons why teachers and parents should appreciate the extent of this strangeness at the cognitive level for the newcomer to school. (At the affective, emotional level, that uneasiness is well appreciated, and in all the schools I worked in very strenuous efforts were made by teachers to diminish it.) The claim that teachers require more than sympathetic appreciation, that their need is for explicit understanding of the processes of classroom interaction is a different one and has still to be established.

The case for understanding, by teachers, of systematic descriptions of classroom discourse

There are, I believe, at least two factors that support this claim, and some suggestions, implied or supposedly implied, that are weak by contrast, and rarely applicable. A claim can be made for a serious, methodical approach to classroom interaction irrespective of whether it is linguistically motivated. This is quite a strong claim, and since it is very generally inclusive, can be stated first.

Teachers are the products of the educational system in which they work. What they experienced and internalised as pupils constitutes a body of knowledge on which they draw heavily and constantly throughout their professional lives. How indispensable that body of knowledge is is evident to anyone who considers the truly daunting prospect of functioning as a teacher in a culture very different from that in which one was educated. There are hazards entailed. One of these is the narrow range of experience for the individual who goes from school to college and returns to school: this has been often discussed. Another, related, hazard is the likelihood that a profession thus educated may unwittingly become a conservative force so strong as to be virtually immovable — one for which change of any but a superficial sort may become, in a literal sense, unthinkable. One powerful safeguard against such conservatism is the introduction into the training process of modes of reflecting upon recent and current experience that identify it as a possible subject of study, assist the individual teacher to distance herself from her experiences and the assumptions derived from it, and provide a conceptual framework and a vocabulary for discussion and criticism. These are necessary purposes, and while it can be argued that a linguistically motivated model of classroom discourse can offer exactly these advantages, I do not think the claim should be made that it is unique in this respect. Some part of the body of work, discussed in chapter 2 above, and motivated by concern for teacher effectiveness, has a well-established place in many pre-service and in-service courses designed for teachers. Its relevance is generally accepted, and its inclusion is highly compatible with current concern that the work of teachers, and of the education system more generally, should be publicly accountable. Coding systems, which have proliferated in great numbers, offer a tool for identifying recurring elements in the unmanageable welter of data that the future teacher perceives when, usually at a quite early stage of training he or she is required to go into the classroom not as a pupil (who can expect his attention to be directed), but as an observer. The most widely used of the available coding systems, Flanders Interaction Analysis Coding, makes a methodical approach possible, claims some degree of reliability between even inexperienced observers, and between observations made by the same observer on different occasions, and has the practical advantage of being rapidly learned, since there are only ten categories to memorise and operate. The observer watches the classroom as if he were watching a film, in which he knows that the life and movement he sees is an illusion brought about by the rapid succession of still frames, any one of which can be halted and isolated for examination. At intervals of three seconds he stops the film, in imagination, and assigns what he sees to one of the ten categories. Six of these refer to teacher and three to pupil activity, and a tenth, 'noise or confusion', allows for the categorisation of what would otherwise be unidentifiable.

At the conclusion it is possible to calculate quickly, and to display, the differing frequencies of occurrence of classroom behaviour identified and classified by the observer, and (by a calculation only a little more elaborate) the frequency with which particular sequences of two sorts of interaction were noticed. The categories include both verbal and non-verbal interaction, though there is an assumption that verbal activity is in some important sense central and representative. The time-bound character of the system is arbitrary, in the sense that it does not correspond to anything in the experience of the participants. There is no reason why anything significant should occur at intervals of three seconds. It simply happens to be the case that an observer at work in real time, that is to say without the use of audio or video tape, and the opportunity of repeated and intensive study of the record, cannot easily note his observations more frequently than that, and may under-use his time if he does so less frequently. From the display of the results it is possible to document, and to claim objectivity for, inferences like these: that teachers usually talk more than pupils, though the balance shifts between teachers and varies with topics and with organisation, and that in some classes particular sequences occur very frequently. Because Flanders's system allows broad, quick, convincing demonstration of fairly straightforward statements about the extent of pupil participation, it has proved to be very useful in in-service and subsequent training. To what extent pupils are taking part is something that is not easily estimated, and about which it is easy to be misled; teachers often do not recognise that they are talking beyond the limits of their hearers' attention. FIAC attributes importance to the short-term succession of linguistic and non-linguistic events, to what follows what, but that is as far as it goes towards the recognition of structure. It does not explain or account for sequences. Its function is to make possible the improvement of performance within a framework of established conventions and assumptions.

Its use avoids some of the disadvantages of unguided observation. This can at worst be trivial, anecdotal, self-indulgent and unrepresentative. It need be none of these things. It has a well-established place in the professional education of teachers, it is the tool most readily accessible to teachers in the classroom, and is in fact a tool that nobody seriously interested in classroom processes can dispense with. At best, participant observation, carefully and methodically planned and carried out, displays a very high degree of fidelity to the actual occurrence, and admits of great sensitivity in interpretation. Since it requires little more than the presence of an observer, who may have a participant role in addition, the disturbance to the processes being observed is minimal. It does not require an elaborate apparatus of previous knowledge. It is the natural history of the classroom, pre-theoretical both in the sense that it does not claim to explain what is observed by relating it to a body of knowledge, and in the sense that it is antecedent to theory. It gives rise to reports and accounts readily accessible to anyone interested in children's development during the years of schooling. There are serious reasons why the use of participant observation should not be disparaged as a mode of research that has a significant role in the pre-service and continuing education of teachers.

The case for careful observation, by teachers, of the classroom interaction of which they are part rests on the critical detachment, almost impossible to attain without it, and on the recognition it makes possible that generalisations having wide applicability, though not easily arrived at and requiring care in application, are none the less possible to attain. Recognisable regularities can be discerned, and these persist in classes that differ on all sorts of dimensions. 'It all depends on the individual', or 'no two schools are alike' are cries of frustration at the difficulty of arriving at generalisations that can be a basis for the making of principled decisions. They are not literal statements of the case. While there is obviously a sense in which every teacher, pupil, and class is unique, yet the relations between and among them are of such a sort that what they have in common is substantial, important, and capable of being made explicit.

The question that has to be asked is what additional advantage, or what advantage in a unique degree is to be had from a description and a coding system that is, unlike those considered so far, linguistically principled? Is the added expenditure of time that such a description entails justified by the results of its use? Since the remainder of the book constitutes in effect an attempt to come to terms with this question I shall offer at this point no more than a brief indication of the stance that is taken. The significant advantage seems to me to be this: a linguistically principled description accepts what is elsewhere implied without discussion, that while it is obvious that a variety of modes of non-verbal and non-vocal communication are in use in class-rooms these are subordinate to the central and most significant means by which teaching and learning occur, that is to situated language use. A sociolinguistic approach offers the single best hope of understanding the processes and the problems that occur in the course of it, not only to the discourse of the classroom, the teachers' and the pupils' understanding of each other, their developing understanding of written texts, their developing ability to produce written texts, teachers' initiation of and response to the texts they produce. A broad under-standing of spoken interaction that does not isolate it from the other varieties of language use in which speakers engage, or from the other

language-related activities that are part of the learning process, seems to
me likely to be productive of better-informed decisions than understanding more narrowly based. Time spent in engaging with the linguistic
study of classroom discourse seems to be time spent economically,
since it constitutes a start made in sociolinguistic studies, an incursion
(and for some teachers and future teachers an appropriate initial
incursion) into a currently developing area, some substantial parts of
which have a bearing upon professional needs and interests. Something
like this seems to be implied by Dell Hymes's (1972c) claim, made in
introducing a collection of essays descriptive of language use in
classrooms:

> The problem of the functions of language in the classroom is a
> challenge and an opportunity for the advancement of linguistics
> itself. Studying language in the classroom is not really 'applied
> linguistics'; it is really basic research. Progress in understanding
> language in the classroom is progress in linguistic theory. (p. xviii)

TAD as a contribution to the understanding of situated discourse

Sustained efforts at uncovering the linguistic regularities that constitute
the structure of classroom discourse have been rare and partial. The
sense is everywhere in *TAD* that new ground is being broken. This was
justified at the time of publication, and is further supported by the
extent of the work of revision, criticism, and expansion that has gone
on since and continues at the time of writing. (Coulthard and Brazil,
1979; Stubbs and Robinson, 1979; Berry, 1981). The authors take up a
well-defined stance in relation to educational concerns. They express a
hope that, in the long term, their work may have a bearing on teachers'
understanding of the spoken texts they produce in interaction with
pupils that will affect, in beneficial ways, the quality of pupils' classroom experience. In particular, they hope that by making available to
teachers a more sophisticated understanding of something so central as
language use to the process of education, to improve the quality of
professional training available to them. They do not claim extensive, or
recent, schoolteaching experience. The empirical work undertaken with
their direct supervision to provide a data base for the initial stages of
their work was quite limited. They refrain from detailed advice, criticisms, or suggestions addressed to teachers. In fact they assume the
viewpoint traditionally associated with linguistic studies, that their job

is descriptive and explanatory; that language users, at the level of discourse as at any other level, know very well what they are doing, that there can be no *linguistic* basis for criticism or advice or for prescription generally. Where a claim to prescribe is made, its real basis will be found not to relate to linguistic factors at all, but to those of social control. Reviewers of the book in the educational (as distinct from the linguistic) journals predictably found such a viewpoint unsympathetic, and reacted in a baffled and generally negative way. There are in the book hints, but no more (pp. 112-13), of dissatisfaction with the position taken up, and a suggestion, at the least, that however necessary it may be as a safeguard against too early and too optimistic conclusions, it cannot be indefinitely sustained.

Their model of classroom discourse is designed to account for the structure of texts having these characteristics; they are spoken (though of course they can be recorded and transcribed for purposes of detailed study, including coding). They are conversational texts, produced by interaction of speakers, and are well described as texts of multiple authorship. They occur in specific, describable situations. Classrooms are institutionalised places, set up to serve the purposes of learning and teaching, though of course these activities go on, and didactic discourse occurs, outside their walls. Virtually everyone in our society and those like it has extensive experience of didactic discourse and most people share the assumption that, by contrast with the fragmentary and desultory character of conversations in more informal settings, that typical of classrooms is orderly and purposeful. It was the intention of the Birmingham team that an explanatory model of its structure should be no more than a beginning, and that they should go out to examine the discourse of other situations, committee meetings, for example, and diagnostic interviews between doctors and patients, television interviews. These are very briefly discussed in chapter 5 of *TAD* (pp. 115-18). The team were much exercised about what a linguistically motivated model of texts of multiple authorship ought to look like. They formalised the criteria by which they found earlier attempts for it wanting, and by which the success of their own could be measured. These are important and have been quoted at length (Burton, 1981) and can here be briefly summarised. First, such an explanatory account has to be comprehensive, not selective. Unless it enables you to say something about *all* the data, it cannot say anything explanatory, as distinct from descriptive, about any of it. The alternative to a comprehensive model is an assembly of observations about the topic, which may of course be interesting, sensitive and thought-provoking, but cannot claim the status of an explanatory model. In fact this criterion is not so difficult to meet as it might appear to be, since a waste basket category (like Flanders's category 10) is perfectly allowable. Second, the descriptive categories must come to a stop. The model must be finite. So long as the examination of every fresh sample of text requires the analyst to construct new descriptive categories, you have work in progress, but not a model. Third, there have to be clear criteria by which particular items can be assigned to their classification. This is a practical necessity of course. The use of any classification system has to be learnable by those who are not concerned with its design. But it is a theoretical requirement too. There is no room, in the process of assigning data to categories, for 'feel' or 'hunch'. These are just names for the operation of unclear criteria, which cannot be verbalised, and for that reason cannot be scrutinised or checked by other analysts, or by the same analyst at a later stage. These are criteria that apply to any descriptive system. The fourth is distinctively linguistic and derives from the nature of language. There must be at least one combination that the system disallows. At no level of language is it the case that 'anything goes'. If it seems to be so, then it is certain that the structure, the very thing which it is the linguists' business to describe, is not being made explicit. In some areas of language the idea that there are some combinations that *look* as if they should be possible but are not is more familiar than at the level of discourse. It is easy to agree that no native speaker of English ever says 'blind three mice', and that no manufacturer, requiring a new English name for a product, calls it 'Sboosh'. These are just not allowable combinations at the level of group structure or at that of consonant combination in initial positions, respectively. A model of discourse that describes structure must disallow some combinations. If no comparable constraints are seen to operate, then either the structure has not been described or it is not linguistic. Examples are needed and *TAD* does not include them. They are offered (in illustration of another point) in Margaret Berry's (1981) discussion of Coulthard and Brazil's classes of move, with the caution that the example must not be interpreted as if it were a continuation of what has gone before. This is a necessary warning. Our resistance to disallowed combinations is so strong that we spontaneously supply what is needed to put right the ill-formed sequence.

*Teacher: A main clause?
Student: Right.
Teacher: What kind of clause is the first clause? (pause)

Teacher: Yes?
*Student: Right.
Teacher: Is the second clause a main clause? (p. 9)
(Note: Asterisks indicate forms that do not occur.)

Any user of English, irrespective of the extent of his familiarity with classrooms, recognises something very odd about each of these exchanges. Clearly the strangeness has nothing to do with vocabulary or grammar. Each is, in discourse terms, ill-formed. 'Right' may realise the marker of a boundary exchange, signalling the start of a new trans-action or the evaluation of a response. Neither is a possibly well-formed responding move by a student to an initiating move on the part of a teacher. Nor could it possibly be succeeded by a reinitiation by the teacher. The rules of discourse disallow boundary exchanges by pupils and normally disallow feedback moves by pupils. (Apparent exceptions, where pupils are occasionally required by the teacher to evaluate each others' contributions are not real exceptions simply because such an exercise has to be deliberately set up and pupils' evaluations legitimised by the teacher.) It would seem reasonable to expect that in the discourse of teachers and their youngest pupils examples of unmistakably ill-formed discourse would occur very often. This is not the case, but they do occur, as in the following, where an eliciting move is followed by another initiating move, this time a directing move by a pupil. Before the teacher has noticed, a second child comes in with the expected right answer:

Teacher: You think. What colour is it?
1st pupil: Read that one!
2nd pupil: Red.

Examples like this are, in my recorded and transcribed text (and in my experience), not readily found. In part, this may well be because mis-understandings that are most simply explained as lexical are, as one would expect, very frequent, and they sometimes make judgments about the well-formedness or its contrary of exchanges difficult to establish. Their rarity has however a more interesting explanation. From many possible examples I quote two where an eliciting move by the teacher is followed not by the expected response but by an inform-ing move on the part of one of the pupils. A lesson in the recognition and naming of shapes was in progress, and the children were asked to pick shapes from a central container and identify them. Not all the children were easily able to see or reach the shapes and the teacher asked:

Can you reach them?

and got in reply from the child:

It's like money.

A little later, the teacher, anxious to establish the term *circle*, asked a question, extending her eliciting move by a *clue*, but again she got an informing move by a pupil in place of the expected answering move:

Teacher: D'you know what name we call a round shape like that?
    a s. . . .
Pupil: It's like an egg!

Teachers have a regular strategy for handling ill-formed discourse of this sort. On the first occasion this teacher said:

Yes. It's like a fifty penny piece, isn't it?

and, moments later,

Not *quite* the shape of an egg.

What she does, on each occasion, is treat the initiative as if it were a response and evaluate it. This strategy effects, so to speak, a rapid repair to the discourse. Pupil initiatives that do not relate to procedures, and are unpredictable in character, momentarily remove control of the discourse from the teacher, but no more than momentarily. Teachers can, and regularly do, notice at once that the discourse is slipping, and make a rapid retrospective adjustment to combinations they recognise as not allowed.

TAD as a contribution to our understanding of classrooms

The Birmingham model goes a long way towards meeting the criteria developed in association with it — further, Coulthard (1975) claims, than its predecessors. It is a rank-scale model, developed with an overall systemic model of language. A *unit*, at any rank, is constituted by one or more units of the rank next below. This is most readily explained to someone unfamiliar with the idea by referring to the level of grammar, where at the top of the rank scale is the sentence, made up of one or more clauses. A clause is made up of one or more groups, and a group of one or more words. A word is made up of one or more of the smallest units, morphemes. Of course it is possible to ask what do the topmost units comprise? and what constitute the smallest units? The answers to both questions require us to move out of grammar, and into another level of language, into text for an answer to the first, into phonology for an answer to the second. Apart from the fundamental advantage of securing continuity with a current and developing model, a rank scale has significant practical advantages. It is flexible: if unexpected patterns emerge in the course of study, a new rank can be created to handle them. No rank has more importance than any other, so there is no reason why an analyst should not choose to concentrate on one or two ranks only, if it suits his purposes to be selective. It is compatible with the criteria developed by Halliday in a seminal article (1961) of what a linguistic description should be — though it is fair to say that the significance of this compatibility emerged only with the development of the model, and seems not to have been apparent in the early stages.

The largest linguistic unit in the Birmingham model is the *lesson*. (This is not to be identified with 'lesson' as a period of time in the school day, defined by bells, which may include more than one entire unit of teacher-pupil interaction, and other activities as well.) A lesson consists of one or more *transactions*. Transactions are made up of *exchanges* and exchanges of *moves*. Moves are made up of *acts*, and the act is the smallest unit of discourse. The answer to the question, what are the constituent parts of an act, has to be in terms of grammar. Similarly, the answer to the question, what do lessons constitute?, has to move out of the area of language altogether, and give an answer couched in terms of pedagogical units, schemes of work, timetables, and programmes of study. Within the study of classroom discourse the ensuing questions have to be these: what elements of structure are to be found at each rank? what classes realise these elements of structure? In attempting to set out as clearly as I can what these are, I propose to make use of just that flexibility that a rank scale permits its users, and to start, not at the top with the most inclusive unit, nor at the bottom with the smallest, but in the middle, with the exchange and the move, since it is in the middle of the rank scale that the description is best developed, theoretically most complete, and most satisfactory in use. Let us start then with the exchange, which is seen as the fundamental unit of discourse (Coulthard, 1975). There are always two participants, though it is not necessarily the case that the contribution of each of them is realised verbally. Exchanges are fundamental units of all sorts of discourse; questions anticipate answers, instructions expect some indication of compliance, information anticipates some sort of acknowledgment. There is an important sense in which, as language users, we all *know* that this is so, and are aware of some breach of rules when our questions go unanswered, our instructions falls (apparently) on deaf ears, or the person who has been informed about the time of the day, the number of the bus, or the direction he should take, offers no word of acknowledgment in return. In classroom discourse there are two classes of exchange, and they are formally and functionally distinct. *Boundary exchanges* signal the start or (less frequently) the conclusion of a topic. Their function is the organisation of the discourse. *Teaching exchanges* serve an educational purpose. All exchanges between teacher and class fall into one of these two classes. Each consists of a quite small number of elements. Boundary exchanges comprise a *frame* or a *focus* or both. That is to say, a teacher may signal a new departure, for which attention and a fresh set of expectations are alike required from pupils, by using one of a small set of items, 'Now', or 'well', or 'OK', or, in conclusion, 'so', or 'finally'. Or he may provide a subheading having a similar function, 'We're going to be looking at fractions again this morning', or 'I want you to look carefully at the picture on page 37 of your books', or he may do both. The labels, frame for the first, focus for the second, are appropriate and easily remembered. That however is less important than that the criteria for including a particular utterance in either class should be explicit.

Teaching exchanges have either two or three elements of structure. An exchange has to be started, so the first *opening* move is obligatory. Typically, there then follows an *answering* move, and this may be verbal or it may be non-verbal. There is then often a third, *follow-up* move. This last distinguishes classroom discourse sharply from discourse situated elsewhere. This exchange, having two moves, opening and answering could occur anywhere:

What's the time?
Half past four.

If a feedback move were present

Well done.

then the hearer supposes at once classroom setting. Further, he puts upon the question, instead of an interpretation like 'I am not wearing a watch, and need a time check', rather one entirely different, 'It's your turn to demonstrate to me that you can interpret the position of the hands of the clock. Do so.'

Opening, answering and follow-up are elements of structure in teaching exchanges. They are realised by *initiating, response* and *feedback* moves. These too have each a structure, described in terms very familiar to anyone who is acquainted with systemic description at the level of grammar. Some of the elements of structure are obligatory, some are optional. Each move has a *head*, as a rule obligatory, and optional elements, the prehead and the posthead, before and after. These elements of structure are realised by *acts*, and these can be specified. Below the move, at the level of the act, the 1975 description is acknowledged to be less than satisfactory. The number of acts (22 are identified) is rather large. Although the number has been singled out as an objection by critics of the model, it is not in itself particularly difficult for the user of the coding system. Each act is functionally distinct, and the terms used (*marker, starter, elicitation,* and *check,* serve as examples) are readily remembered after some practice. Of these acts, twenty are required for the realisation of elements of structure at the level of the *move.* Two more are distinct in their function; the *loop* is a means of describing what happens when classroom discourse falters, and needs to be taken back to an earlier point. Something, because of interruption or extraneous noise, or momentary inattention, has been missed. There is of course nothing peculiar to classroom discourse about lapses of this sort or repair strategies for them. The other, the *aside,* is required to take account of the things teachers say, to colleagues or pupils or, more frequently, to themselves, that are no part of the classroom discourse, and that pupils know they must ignore, or seem not to hear. The problem with *acts* is not their number; it is simply this, there is no principled reason why the number should not be indefinitely larger. There is a breach here of the author's own criterion of finiteness. There is no way of knowing that the examination of another text might not require the addition of other acts. Later work on the structure of *exchanges* (Coulthard and Brazil, 1979) made possible a reduction of the number of acts that required to be separately identified, and, they claim, a principled reason for identifying ten and no more.

Another difficulty is experienced at the top of the scale. The *lesson* is an unordered series of *transactions.* No suggestion of *disorder* is implied of course; what is meant is that the lucid and methodical arrangements that make a good lesson interesting and assimilable derive from logical or narrative structure, not from discernible and describably linguistic structure. In fact there are quite serious difficulties in regarding a lesson as a linguistic unit at all. In primary and secondary schools, it is certainly an important unit of organisation. Its length is predetermined and is as a rule a compromise among conflicting requirements. It is a device for ensuring that different subjects of the curriculum get a fair share of time and other resources, and that variety and regularity characterise the working day. Most lessons include longer or shorter periods given over to lessons in the sense the word has here, sequences of interaction between the teacher and a class (which may or may not include all the pupils in the room). The lesson as an administrative device is a rather rare occurrence in the earliest stages of education, where subject divisions are fewer and broader, organisation is flexible, and the day is typically divided into sessions by 'natural' breaks, for milk or play, or a midday meal. Within those sessions, sequences of transactions frequently occur, and their length is determined by the teacher's estimate of the span of attention the children can maintain. The teacher has a degree of freedom not usually available to someone teaching older pupils, to direct attention elsewhere and to change the activity. At present we have no description of a lesson as a linguistic unit, but it has to be acknowledged that this is generally true of large sections of situated discourse. Nor is the description of a transaction more than a sketch. It must comprise a preliminary exchange, and that will be a boundary exchange. There must be at least one medial element of structure, realised by a teaching exchange, and there can be any number of these. There may be, but need not be, a terminal exchange – a boundary exchange again. These transactions are unordered again in the sense that the order in which they occur is determined by other factors than linguistic structure.

From the model of classroom discourse developed by the Birmingham team, and here briefly described, a system for coding text is derived. By 'coding' we mean here displaying the analysis of a given sample of transcribed text which the descriptive model makes possible. Obviously those responsible for the model needed to do this, and they include a substantial selection of coded text in *TAD* (chapter 4, pp. 61-90). It is the most obvious way of testing the claim to comprehensiveness. In order to support such a claim, it should be possible to apply the coding system to samples of transcribed text assembled randomly from all sorts of teaching situations, including classes of pupils older and younger than those in the sample that supplied the original data, and including teachers having different experience and educational convictions and dissimilar teaching styles. This is certainly possible, and is illustrated in the concluding section of this chapter where I have followed the layout preferred by the authors of *TAD*, setting out the coded and transcribed text in the form of a grid, so that the elements of structure of each exchange are set out across the page, the moves are divided by vertical and the exchanges by horizontal lines, and a narrow column adjacent to the moves provides for the identification of the acts by which the structure of the moves is realised. This display has the advantage of providing the information offered in a way that is easily read, and in my own use of it I have found that it distinguishes the exchanges, and displays their structure, very satisfactorily. I find it less satisfactory at the level of the move, where it displays the acts (at the head, prehead, and posthead, the second and third being optional) much less clearly. For this purpose the layout employed by Stubbs and Robinson (1979) is preferable. It has the disadvantage of being less compact, and better suited therefore to the quotation and discussion of brief samples of text than to the analysis of substantial sections.

Analysed text

There follows at the conclusion of this chapter a number of samples of text recorded in nursery and reception classes. These are intended to serve two related purposes. One is to furnish illustration of the possibility of coding text that is dissimilar from that which provided the data base of the Birmingham study, and furnished the samples of coded text included in the 1975 study. The other is to support by means of commentary on the analyses the claim implied throughout this chapter and argued on pp. 188-9 above, that the process of coding is productive of insight. If this is generally the case, then it should be true in detail. An attempt is made to indicate observations that are prompted by the analysis and that suggest interesting additional directions of enquiry. These texts have been selected from a much larger body of spoken text, and have been chosen almost randomly. Wherever teachers engaged in interaction with groups, as distinct from assembling them for the purpose of telling a story, or calling the register, the discourse would have served my illustrative purpose. The introductory descriptions in this section serve simply to set the scene and indicate the nature of the activity. The first of these was recorded in a nursery class early in the school term and year, at the end of the morning. It is the start of a singing session which children left when they were fetched by their mothers. The teacher relies on the fact that some songs and rhymes were known to some of the children, and they could and did join in, given a strong lead from her.

The layout of the analysed text closely follows that of Sinclair and Coulthard (1975), pp. 63-110. Where space allows, and generally in the identification of the exchanges and the moves, I have avoided using abbreviations. This has not been possible in identifying the acts, where the following abbreviations have been used:

m.	marker	rea.	react
s.	starter	rep.	reply
ch.	check	P-init.	initiating move by a pupil
el.	elicitation	N.V.	non-verbal response
d.	directive	ack.	acknowledgment
i.	informative	com.	comment
n.	nomination	ev.	evaluation
MS.	meta-statement		

The classes of acts, and the ways in which they are realised, are described in detail in Sinclair and Coulthard (1975), pp. 40-4.

Exchange type	Opening		Answering		Follow-up
boundary	C'mon then. FRAME Let's have a look at everybody. FOCUS	m. ms.			
teaching elicit	Who remembers . . .?	el.			
direct	Sh'we have quiet Sam?	dir. [n.]			
re-initiate	Who remembers baa baa black sheep?	el.	(noise — not transcribable)		

Exchange type	Opening		Answering		Follow-up	
direct	C'mon then. You can all sing that one.	s. d.	(teacher and children sing the rhyme)	rea.		
elicit	Can we have 'One, two, three, four, five?'	el.	(noise — not transcribable)	rea.		
direct	Show me five fingers then.	d.	N.V.	rea.		
elicit	One, two, three, four, five.	el.	two, three, four, five. . . .			
elicit	Can anybody. . .?	el.	yes . . . yes.	rep.	Not Jack and Jill a proper song. . . not a nursery rhyme . . . a song.	ev.
direct	C'mon then. Ready . . . wide arms.	s. d.	(Children and teacher sing the chorus)	rea.	Good. . . .	ev.
elicit	What else can you remember?	el.	(noise — not transcribable)			
elicit	Who had a poorly dolly?	el.				
	Where's her dolly?	el.				

Exchange type	Opening		Answering		Follow-up	
direct	C'mon let me see.	d.	(Children and teacher sing 'Miss Polly had a dolly')			
direct	Ashley, will you join in with us please?	d. [n.]				
elicit	Who rides on a pony?	el.				
re-initiate	Who rides on a pony?	el.	(noise, from which emerges) me! me!			
re-initiate	In the song who rides on a pony?	el.	(noise)			
re-initiate	Who can ride on a pony?	el.	(noise – on which the teacher imposes the required answer) A cowboy!			
P-init.	(inaudible)		*Do* you?	rep.		
direct	C'mon then.	d.	(the teacher and pupils sing 'On my pony see me ride')			
direct	C'mon then.	d.	N.V.	rea.		

Exchange type	Opening		Answering		Follow-up	
boundary	Right. FRAME	m.				
elicit	Any more songs that you'd like to sing?	el.	(babel of noise from which emerges) Humpty Dumpty!	rep.	All right we'll sing Humpty Dumpty first, and then we'll sing. . . .	ack.
re-initiate	What's yours Janet?	el. [n.]			(inaudible)	com.
elicit	Where's your Humpty Dumpty sitting on a wall?	el.				
re-initiate	Is he all ready to fall off?	el.				
re-initiate	Is he a bit wobbly?	el.				
P-init.	I got *two* Humpty Dumpties!				Oh you can't have *two* Humpty Dumpties. He has to sit on a wall.	ev. com.
direct	Are you ready then?	el.	(children and teacher sing the rhyme)			
boundary	Well, all I can	m.				

Exchange type	Opening		Answering		Follow-up	
	say is you've got *very* funny eggs, because all the eggs in *my* house have got round bottoms so they wobble over if you put them on the table! FOCUS	i.				
elicit	Do yours?	el.	no . . . no . . . no . . .	rep.		
elicit	Do you have eggs in your house?	el.				
re-initiate	They stand still if you put them in an egg cup, don't they?	el.				
re-initiate	You don't put an egg cup on the wall, do you?	el.				
re-initiate	Humpty Dumpty	el.	(noise) no			

Exchange type	Opening		Answering		Follow-up	
	didn't have an egg cup, did he?					
direct	Are you ready?	el.				
direct	Shsh	d.				
direct	Yes . . . go on.	d.				
direct	Are you ready to sing about David?	el.	Yes.	rep.		
elicit	How many little boys were there called David?	el.	One.	rep.	One	
direct	Neil and Dean, turn round and join in with us.	d. [n.]	N.V.	rea.		
elicit	Who's this?	el.				
direct	Go on then sit down Sharon, quickly.	d. [n.]	(teacher and pupils sing 'Little Peter Rabbit's got a fly upon his nose')			
direct	Come'n sit down Sharon-	d. [n.]				

Exchange type	Opening		Answering		Follow-up	
	er-Louise there's a good girl.					
inform	We're not doing any more pictures today.	i.				
inform	You'll do another one tomorrow.	i.				
elicit	All right?	ch.				
direct	Come and sit down.	dir.				
direct	Come on, come and sit down.	dir.	N.V.	rea.	That's it.	ev.
elicit	What has it been doing today?	el.	Raining.	rep.	Raining.	ev.
elicit	And what do we sometimes get with rain?	el.	(babel of sound — not transcribable)			
re-initiate	No . . . a noise	el.	Teacher: thunder	rep.	Yes.	ev.
direct	Are you ready?	dir.	(teacher and pupils sing 'I hear thunder')		That thunder carries on an awful long	

Exchange type	Opening		Answering		Follow-up	
					time.	
direct	Dean and Neil, I shan't tell you again to turn round and sit up please.	d. [n.]				
direct	Come on, sit up please.	d.	N.V.	rea.	Thank you.	ack.
elicit	Hello. Have you come to look for your sister?	el.	Not yet.	rep.	Not yet.	ack.
elicit	Where's one little finger?	el.				
elicit	How many?		(inaudible)	rep.	Four. Good.	ack. ev.
elicit	How many Amanda?	el. [n.]	Five.	rep.	Five.	ack.
direct	Ready?	d.				
elicit	Mark, what would you like to sing?	el. [n.]	(inaudible)	rep.	Oh, not again. We'll sing that again tomorrow.	ev. com.
elicit	All right. What would	s.	(noise, in which can be			

Exchange type	Opening		Answering		Follow-up	
	you like to sing?	el.	discerned) 'Jack and Jill', 'Mary Mary'		Mary Mary.	ack.
direct	All right.	d.	(children and teacher sing)		Very good I didn't know you knew that one.	ev. com.
elicit	Do you know the one about the little star?	el.	'Twinkle Twinkle'	rep.	'Twinkle Twinkle'	ack.
direct	Are you ready?	el.	N.V.	rea.		
direct	Mark, are you ready?	el. [n.]	(teacher and pupils sing 'Twinkle Twinkle little star')			
elicit	Neil, can you sing with your mouth shut up?	el. [n.]	N.V.	rep.	You weren't singing then were you, 'cos your mouth was closed up.	ack.
direct	You sit down there, and join in with us.	d.				
elicit	Who comes out to play?	el.	Me! Georgie Porgie.	rep. rep.	No. That's the little	ev.

Exchange type	Opening		Answering		Follow-up	
					girls who come out to play there.	com.
elicit	Who comes out to play?	el.				
	Boys and . . .?	el.				
direct	Are you ready to sing that one then?	el.	(teacher and children sing 'Boys and girls come out to play')			

In this first extract there is already an approximation to a well-formed classroom discourse. It is no more than an approximation — there is, for example no *bidding*, no *cues*, and no subsequent *nomination* of one speaker from among several. Still, it is, even at this stage, recognisable and analysable. Further, the teacher assumes that these young pupils will know that a question, or a statement, can have a *directive* function (though disobedience persuades her to the use of an unmistakable *imperative*). While the children's answering moves are often hesitant and confused, they seem in no doubt *when* a verbal and when a non-verbal answering move is expected. Their teacher expects, and tolerates, answers that are unexpected or inappropriate, or indeed, inaudible, and she selects from the babel one answer that satisfies her, or imposes the response she hoped to hear, in very much the same way as the mothers, in Snow's (1972) study, interpreted a sound or a look or a movement on the part of the baby as if it were a turn at talking that could properly elicit another in reply. To the teacher, who has herself been exposed to the educational system of this country (and to no other) it seems natural to make virtually all the *initiating moves*, to expect from the children a subordinate and responding role, and to create a framework that virtually ensures it.

The children seem (collectively) well aware that they have to respond to the teacher's initiatives. They are however very inexperienced pupils, and it is noticeable that the task of guessing at the answer that the teacher expects is sometimes too difficult for them. In reply to the question 'Who rides on a pony?', there are cries of 'Me! Me!' and in reply to 'Who comes out to play?' the same insistent 'Me!', as if it were natural, when there is no way of knowing what is the expected answer, to resort to an assertion of one's identity and presence. No hands are raised, and the teacher does not interpret 'Me' as a *bid*. Briefer examples serve to illustrate other observations. All of them relate to that part of each day when teachers interact with groups of seated children in what was seen as a work setting.

The following excerpt is the text of a first meeting between a teacher in the reception class and a group fresh from the nursery. These pupils, all rising 5, were understandably feeling very shy and uncertain what was expected of them. Their contribution to the discourse is minimal. For all that, the text made by teacher and pupils is analysable, and this confirms my belief that it is the teacher's certainty about what constitutes well-formed discourse that makes it so.

Exchange type	Opening		Answering		Follow-up	
boundary	I tell you what we'll ask you . . . your name. FOCUS	ms.				
direct	I wonder if you . . . when we ask you your name, you could be very big, and stand up and tell us your name so we could have a good look at you. I wonder	s.				

Exchange type	Opening		Answering		Follow-up	
	who's big enough to do that? Sam, I wonder could you stand up and tell us who you are?	d. [n.]	No.	rep.		
inform	You're Sam.	i.				
elicit	Sam who?	el.				
re-initiate	Do you know?	el.	Sam B–.	rep.	You're Sam B–!	ack.

Even these young pupils were not always docile respondents. They did volunteer information. *Pupil-initiatives* occurred, and when they did, teachers typically handled them as if they were *answering moves* in relation to an unspoken, but clearly understood initiating move from her. Teachers did not usually offer a *reply*: they responded by *acknowledgment* or *evaluation*.

Exchange type	Opening		Answering		Follow-up	
P-init.	We got a goldfish called Beauty.	i.			That's nice, thank you Dawn.	ack. ev.

Immediately after came a *boundary move*, at the start of a *transaction* that was to launch that afternoon's story of *The Three Little*

Cats. From one of the children came a reply that from an older pupil would certainly be regarded as impertinent; indeed not all teachers would excuse it in a 5-year-old. *This* teacher had her own way of handling it, that preserved, in a manner apparently effortless, the smoothness of the social interaction in the classroom.

Exchange type	Opening		Answering		Follow-up	
boundary	Today I thought we'd have a story about some cats. FOCUS	ms.				
teaching elicit	Have you got a cat at home?	el.				
re-initiate	Have you?	el.	Miaow!	rep.	Oh yes, that's the noise they make, isn't it?	ack. com.

There is a moment here of the sort the inexperienced teacher dreads. What this pupil offers is *not* a well-formed *answering move*, and he probably knows it. If the others notice that he gets away with it, and set up in imitation, there will be a moment of wild, and probably noisy, defiance, and the teacher will be obliged to assert her authority with a corresponding loudness. At best, her image of herself as someone who exerts effortless and unchallenged control will be shaken. At worst, she will have the embarrassment of attracting the attention of her colleagues. That is not, however, what happens. By the comment that follows her acknowledgment of the answering move, this teacher retrospectively *changes* the initiating move in such a way as to enable her to accept what the pupil said as a (just) satisfactory answer.

The final example is part of a reading lesson in the reception class, and must be reckoned something of a landmark in the lives of the children involved, since it was their first introduction to their reading scheme, *Breakthrough to Literacy*. The teacher used a large colour photograph of a house, and it was her intention that 'house' should be the first word the children learned to recognise. In the event, their attention was caught by details that were irrelevant to her purpose, and the words they supplied were not those she proposed to begin by teaching.

Exchange type	Opening		Answering		Follow-up	
teaching elicit [n.]	Joanne, what do *you* think is in the picture?	el. n.	A bungalow.	rep.	You think it's a bungalow as well Joanne do you? Two Joannes think it's a bungalow.	ack. n. com.
elicit	What do you think Neil?	el. [n.]				
re-initiate	What can you see in the picture?	el.				
re-initiate	Tell me what you can see.	el.	There's none upstairs.	i.	There's no upstairs. That's right.	ack. ev.
P-init.	I think it's a house.	i.			You think it's a house.	ack.
elicit	What do you think?	el.				
re-initiate	What can you	el.	Bung.	rep.	You think	ack.

Exchange type	Opening		Answering		Follow-up	
	see in my picture, Simon?	[n.]			it's a bungalow. That's the proper word for it isn't it, a bungalow.	com.
elicit	What does a bungalow mean Joanne?	el. [n.]	Er – don't know.	rep.		
elicit	D'you know what it means?	el.	(inaudible) – got pushchairs.	rep.		
elicit	Pardon? Got pushchairs?	l. el.				
re-initiate	Where's the pushchairs?	el.	There.	rep.	It's just outside, isn't it. Yes.	ack.
elicit	Did you see that pushchair, er, Simon?	el. [n.]				
P-init.	It 'asn't got an upstairs but it 'as got a downstairs.	i.			That's right. That's what bungalow means Joanne. It hasn't got an upstairs	ev. com. [n.]

Exchange type	Opening		Answering		Follow-up	
					it just has a downstairs.	
P-init.	It 'as got downstairs. You'd have to sit (sleep?) downstairs.	i.			That's right. Yes. Um. It's *similar* to a house, isn't it? It's *like* a house, but it	ev. com.
boundary	Now. FRAME Neil.	m. [n.]				
P-init.	It hasn't got an upstairs.	i.			That's right.	ack.
boundary	Now. FRAME	m.				
elicit	Neil, can you tell me about your house?	el. [n.]				
re-initiate	Is your house like this?	el.	No.	rep.	No, I'm asking Neil, love.	ev. com. [n.]
elicit	What's your house like Neil?	el.				
re-initiate	Can you tell me about your house?	el.				

Exchange type	Opening		Answering		Follow-up	
re-initiate	What's your house made of?	el.	Bricks.	rep.	Your house is made of bricks.	ack.
elicit	D'you remember the story of the three little pigs?	el.				
	What were *their* houses made of?	el.	Straw.	rep.	*One* was made of straw.	ev.
			One was made of twigs.	rep.	One was made of twigs.	ack.
			One was made of bricks.	rep.	One was made of bricks.	ack.
elicit	Which was the *strongest* house?	el.	Bricks.	rep.	Bricks.	ack.
elicit	Is your house made of bricks Joanne?	el. [n.]	Yes.	rep.	Your house is made of bricks.	ack.
elicit	And yours?	el.	Yes.			
elicit	*Right*! FRAME					
P-init. Teacher	And Dean's is! Pardon?	i. l.				

Exchange type	Opening		Answering		Follow-up	
P-init.	And Dean's is!	i.			And Dean's is. Oh, I'm glad of that.	ack.

As these children begin to learn about literacy, it appears that they have already learned what it is to be a pupil, and in general terms, how they are expected to respond to their teacher. That learning is still incomplete, though. In the extract analysed above, Neil continues the topic of the bungalow that is distinguished from a house by not having an upstairs *after* the teacher has signalled her readiness to start a fresh transaction. He is allowed to finish, although the contribution made to the earlier topic at a point where she is ready to move to a new one must be perceived by the teacher as an interruption. She deals with it quite gently, but the fact that she does not pursue the matter, offers the speaker a second opportunity to recognise that *that* topic is finished with. The teacher *nominates* a great deal. Nearly every question is addressed to a particular pupil, where in a class of older children it is more usual to allow *bidding* for the right to speak. Given that this series of exchanges was recorded very early in the term, it is possible that the teacher is deliberately identifying the pupils in an effort to impress their names early and indelibly on her own memory. It is also likely that this is done in order to get the children to recognise that everyone normally *has* a turn. One apparently acceptable response is negatively evaluated, and the speaker is reminded that it was Neil, not he, who was asked. He is here deliberately taught that knowing the answer is not enough, it is being *nominated* that confers the right to speak. The teacher notices (at the beginning of the sequence) what is frequently apparent to the observer: that where an answer seems to be acceptable it is likely to be imitated — not always appropriately. For some children, doing what someone else has done, and what the teacher has been seen to approve, is a frequent learning strategy. This is not of course to say that it is a very satisfactory one.

These excerpts exemplify, not perfectly well-formed classroom discourse, but a working approximation to it, and the number of examples could be indefinitely multiplied. They are representative of the text that was regularly created when the teachers assumed control (as distinct from supervision), when the pupils were assembled and seated in larger or smaller groups, and when the teacher saw the business in hand as an educational task. Much of the time in the nursery, and some of the time in the reception class, was quite differently employed, and the range of language use in which the children engaged was correspondingly different. They quarrelled and teased and made believe. They chattered, plotted mischief, and bragged. Their utterances were not then usually monosyllabic, and they naturally and commonly took initiatives. The responding role of the pupil, far from being as I had initially supposed, something *difficult* of achievement, seemed to represent no more than part of the range of language use with which they came to school already equipped. It seemed as if here was further evidence that 'children prove in every instance to know more than we previously believed' (Bates, 1979). Further it was a role of a limited kind, defined in relation to that of the teacher. She took the initiatives, decided the topics, and remained all the time in control. *Her* consciousness of the kind of discourse proper to the classroom went a very long way towards creating and sustaining it. How the reciprocal interaction of pupils and teacher related to learning, or, more generally, to the purposes of early schooling was the question that had next to be examined.

6

Discourse and the processes of early education

The concerns of this chapter are with the relations between well-formed discourse, describable in the terms set out in the preceding pages, and the processes of learning and teaching; between the purposes for which society sets up and maintains schools and classrooms, and the text that is created in the course of what goes on in them. My first concern will be with what is observable of the ways in which young newcomers learn what the rules are. This will involve the examination of passages of recorded and transcribed text, and a selective use of the coding system derived from the Birmingham model already described and illustrated. Second, there is a complementary question to be asked, and more briefly answered: how do *teachers* learn to operate the rules that obtain in their part in the discourse, and to exercise their varied, demanding rights and responsibilities in it? Third, there is a question to be asked about the discourse itself. Does its orderly and rule-governed character derive from the necessities of learning and teaching and does it serve those purposes uniquely well? Or are there other sorts of didactic discourse, still awaiting systematic and linguistically principled description?

The text quoted in this chapter and the last is selected from a very much larger body of recorded and transcribed text, and, like anyone who reflects on some part of the text produced by the operation of learning and teaching processes in which she was engaged as observer or participant, I make the assumption that it is not unrepresentative. If it has interest for other teachers, that interest lies not in any exceptional character, but in its ordinariness. That assumption is a ground rule of most discussions among teachers on educational topics, and the defence I offer is twofold — that nearly all my examples could be many times multiplied by reference to the records from which the selection was made, and that teachers familiar with this age group recognise them as entirely ordinary.

Learning to make responding moves

The provision of opportunities for language development was a constant concern in all the schools in which I worked, and opportunities
for talk were arranged as part of each day's programme. Talk was seen
as a prerequisite of literacy, a prime factor in social and intellectual
development. The following example is an excerpt from an activity
which, in the nursery class in which it was recorded, was known as
'family time'. At a mid-point of each session, each teacher assembled
the group of up to fifteen children that constituted her 'family'. Often
a story provided a talking-point. Sometimes, as in the following series
of exchanges, talk was allowed to develop from an observation by the
teacher:

Teacher: Darren's gone into his new class in school.
Pupil: My sister . . . .
Teacher: Your sister . . . has she gone? Your sister's still in class 4
    or has she gone into a new school?
Pupil: New school . . . .
Teacher: Has she gone into the junior school? Well, isn't that lovely?

Here the teacher seeks to encourage an initially hesitant contribution.
However, we shall never know what we were to hear about the sister,
because the pupil's uncertain initiative was made the starting-point for
a question by the teacher of the sort sometimes termed 'closed', since
no more than a very brief reply is possible. A similar strategy on the
part of a teacher is quoted and analysed in Sinclair and Coulthard's
Towards an Analysis of Discourse (p. 85), where a teacher allows a
child who offers information derived from a children's television
programme to offer it, but rapidly recovers the initiative from her.

The teacher's paraphrase of the reply serves as a feedback to the
pupil. Clearly what she said was acceptable — more than acceptable to
judge by the comment —

    Well, isn't that lovely?

That comment is not altogether easy to interpret. It may relate to
content. Movement to the next stage of the educational process is often
talked about in children's learning as if it represented deserved promo-
tion. It may be intended as a positive comment on the effort made by
the speaker. The exchanges continue:

Teacher: She's got a new uniform . . . blue was it? Blue or grey? She's
   got a new jumper? Or has she got a cardigan?
Pupil: Cardie.
Teacher: Lovely. Lovely.
   Nigel, would you like a piece of apple?
   Anyone want more milk?
   Anyone want a piece of apple? No?
   All right.
   Wouldn't you like to drink yours up like Jason?
   Nigel, would you like to drink your milk all up like Jason's doing?
   You don't want any more?
   Good girl.
   You've got new shoes have you?
   What colour are they Chatinder?
   What colour are Chatinder's shoes?
   Can you remember?
   Black.
   Can you say that?
   You say it then.
Pupil: Black.
Teacher: Good girl.

In the process of providing opportunities for the children to contribute, this teacher established very firmly her adult dominance. She
made successive initiating moves without interruption. Theirs, even
when they were invited and welcome, were liable to be cut short. No
more than a brief response was expected from them, and was sure of
approval. It was hardly surprising that many of the children found
safety in a silence that leaves no trace in the recorded and transcribed
text. Is this then simply an example of what has been observed many
times – that the confidence and fluency of adults may serve to discourage children's conversational efforts, contrary to adult intention?
In a sense it is, but it is possible to pursue the matter further. Pupil
initiatives do occur in well-formed discourse. They are often concerned
with procedural matters. The pupil who makes eliciting moves ('What
do I do when I've finished? Can I borrow a rubber?') is in effect asking
the teacher to give a directive or to repeat one already given. This does
not challenge the teacher's control. If anything it reinforces it. The
teacher who sets out to get children talking, who deliberately makes
space and opportunity for *their* informing moves does something
different. She seems to invite pupils to assume control of the discourse

— but it is unexpectedly difficult for her to relinquish control of the discourse and social control with it more than momentarily. An explicit understanding of the discourse rules would be really helpful to the teacher here by explaining why she feels, and in some sense *is* obliged to recover the initiative from the pupil. Such an understanding might suggest the use of other strategies, offering children less ambiguous opportunities, and serve to rebut the suggestion that seems to be implied that teachers are generally dominating people who find listening to children difficult. What pupils are likely to learn in the course of this sort of conversational interchange is that their part is to provide responses and to do so briefly.

Once the children had settled in the nursery, their teachers regularly spoke as if they already knew what sort of behaviour, verbal and other, is expected of a pupil, but, because they were unfamiliar with their new surroundings, might well need quite frequent reminders. As teachers they were prepared to be appropriately tolerant in their judgment of what was acceptable. They made much use of *prompts* and *clues*. If these were not enough they would supply the response, providing, as they did so, a model of what they were looking for. Examples can readily be found. In this one a teacher has a small group of children engaged in a game that requires the player to match two colour-coded items. The material is designed to teach colour recognition and naming. It is less simple than it appears, since it depends on an unspoken assumption very remote from everyday experience, that (for example) the blue kennel belongs to the dog with the blue collar, and the yellow kite to the girl wearing the yellow dress. Coding displays clearly the degree of perseverance required to teach what sort of answer is expected.

Exchange type	Opening		Answering		Follow-up	
teaching elicit	Which doggie belongs in which kennel?	el.				
re-initiate	Which kennel does *that* doggie	el.	In that one. (pointing to the nearest —	rep.		

Exchange type	Opening		Answering		Follow-up	
	belong in?		not matched for colour)			
re-initiate	Does he?	el.	Yeah.	rep.		
direct	You open it up and see.	dir.		rea.		
elicit	Is that right?		No.			
elicit	Why does *he* belong in the kennel?	el.				
re-initiate	What's the same?	el.	The kennel.	rep.	Yes.	ack.
elicit	But what's the same between that and the kennel, the dog and the . . .?		Blue.	rep.	*Blue*!	ev.

This teacher perseveres until the pupil gives the expected answer, and may well have understood the unstated rules of the game. In such passages of exchange, a look, or a gesture, or even a silence may be interpreted as if it were an attempt at the required answer, and by these means, and not always easily, the teacher discharges what she perceives as her necessary and essential function, that of sustaining the discourse until the appropriate moment comes when, in her judgment, she can discontinue it in favour of another activity or another need. These exchanges, with individuals or with smaller or larger groups, occurred spontaneously or by intention throughout the session. This one occurred during a play period. One of the teachers had given a little girl an account of her own, much older daughter's activities at home and asked what sort of things she did at home. Her hesitant answer was inaudible on the tape, and was perhaps inaudible to her teacher, who pursued the matter with fresh questions.

Teacher: And what else?
Pupil: I have to do the glasses.
Teacher: Making glasses? D'you wash up? Or d'you help Mummy wipe up sometimes? Does Mummy let you wipe up?
Pupil: My Mummy . . . .

It seems to take time for the child to understand that an answer is expected. When it comes, it is the teacher's turn to be puzzled — perhaps at the idea of so young a child handling glassware. When the second, very hesitant reply comes, the little girls starts, falters almost at once into silence, but the teacher almost at once evaluates the partial answer as if it were quite satisfactory.

This is not an untypical conversation. Even in talk with friendly adults, used to children and entirely well disposed towards them, children have only limited rights as participants. A child's turn at talking may be offered and then withdrawn before a hesitant contribution is made. For reasons adults readily appreciate, but which must be supposed quite incomprehensible to children, teachers often feel obliged to engage pupils in talk that has really very little interest for the adult participant. That adult, having nearly all the conversational rights in the interaction has the right to cut it short when the obligation to devote a minimal time to it has been discharged. Children must sometimes experience the exercise of that right as a dismissal, but they cannot effectively challenge adult decisions.

If the rights in conversational interaction belong to the teacher, so too do the responsibilities, including the paramount responsibility of sustaining the interaction for a length of time that was sometimes, but not always, for the individual teacher to determine. This was not always easy. From time to time the eliciting moves made by the teacher got in response a babel of confused sound, on which some sort of order had to be imposed before a feedback move could be made. The passage quoted and analysed above (p. 104) illustrates some of the ways in which one teacher did this, and some of the learning made available to pupils in the process. When in the course of the song-session, her eliciting move

Who rides on a pony?

got not the expected answer, but a variety of answers, not clearly audible, she ignored all of them, and reinitiated her question

In *the song* who rides on a pony?,

deftly supplying the assistance that is required to secure the expected answer, 'a cowboy'.

The analogy of a game is inescapable. The teacher did what adult players do. Well versed in her own part, she played it fully and encouraged the children to play theirs so far as they could. Where children, being inexperienced players, fail to make the expected moves, adults supply the assistance that is needed, or, if that is not enough, supply the missing move so that the game can proceed without inter-ruption. Approval is warm, unmistakable, and neither so critical nor so discriminating as it will later become. Since nearly all children want and need to interact with adults and to secure their approval, these are very effective strategies for ensuring what is, unexpectedly so evident in early classroom interaction, an overall, though in detail an approximate, conformity to expectation. Children seem, as a group, to learn what is wanted almost immediately, often in the course of a single session. The following set of exchanges illustrates the rapidity of the process. It was recorded within a week of the start of the school year. At the onset the teacher supplied the answers to her own questions, all of which related to a story she had just read to her class. In the course of the exchanges the children appeared to identify the requirements they initially failed to understand, and their silences, and their hesitant and inaudible replies, gave way to answers modelled on those. Several reinitiating moves were needed.

Teacher: I wonder what else they learnt?
   What did they tell Auntie Doris?
   What did they tell Auntie Doris about?

There was no answer, and the teacher tried again, with reminders of the story as clues to the required responses:

Teacher: She'd got all her medicines and tablets locked up in a
   cupboard, safely out of the way. What had she left in the wrong
   cupboard? Where somebody can get at them?

Again, no answer from any of the children, so the teacher supplied an answer for them, before initiating another series of eliciting moves. Again, in the absence of responding moves from any of the pupils, she supplied them.

Teacher: Yes. The bleach and the scouring powder. So she put those
    safely away, didn't she? What are these?

At this point, the teacher indicated an illustration, and one of the children attempted to respond. However the teacher either failed to hear, or disregarded the tentative response, and again she supplied the answer to her own question:

Teacher: Tablets. What mustn't we do with tablets? We mustn't eat
    them, must we?
Pupil: No.
Teacher: If we find anything that looks like sweets, and we're not
    sure, we have to go and ask Mummy, don't we?
Pupil: Yes.

These questions that allow of yes or no as brief, but quite acceptable answers, are altogether easier. The teacher continued:

Teacher: Oh but you have to ask Mummy. You mustn't eat anything
    without asking Mummy if it's all right, must you?

None of the children assented to this despite what seems a clear indication that they are expected to do so.

Teacher: Let's have a look. What're found here? A bike and . . .?

No reply, so the teacher continued:

            . . . and side-car, haven't they?
    Yes. What are they doing here?
    What were they doing?

One pupil seemed at this point to understand what was wanted, and to have felt confident enough to supply it audibly and distinctly:

Pupil: Riding on it.
Teacher: They were riding on it, weren't they?

Exchange type	Opening		Answering		Follow-up	
teaching elicit	What were they doing?	el.	Riding on it.	rep.	They were riding on it, weren't they?	ev.
teaching elicit	What happened to poor Topsy?	el.				
re-initiate	What happened?	el.	Got locked in.	rep.	She did.	ack.
teaching elicit	And what did Uncle Frank say? You must never. . . .	el. cl.	Teacher: Shut yourself into anything while you're playing.	rep.		
teaching elicit	What was their reward for being such good, sensible children? They went for a ride in a. . . .	el. cl.	Tractor.	rep.	Tractor, yes.	ack.

In such exchanges it appeared that the pattern of classroom discourse was rapidly and effectively established. Observations like this run contrary to any expectation that complex kinds of behaviour will be gradually mastered over a period of time, and that young children, for whom economical generalities are without much meaning, will be obliged to learn slowly. These observations are so familiar that it is natural enough to bring to the study of the processes of learning to participate in classroom discourse, the expectations they create. Natural, but misleading. The rapidity of the language acquisition process was, in the 1960s, so much insisted on that its assertion now at once evokes scepticism. Where the enquiring observer's suppositions about a process include a consciousness of its complexity, he is very ready to be impressed by the rapidity with which the learning of it is accomplished. This was my experience. What I observed indicated that learning to interact with a teacher in expected and appropriate ways is not an extended process attained by discernible stages. Where motivation is compelling, and circumstances are favourable, the limited understanding needed to respond adequately is quickly acquired by some members of a new class. Mistakes however, do occur, and it is worth some closer examination of these, since the processes by which meanings are negotiated are often most clearly seen when they are not easily accomplished, and no more than partially successful. Mismatch of knowledge, experience and expectation between teacher and pupil is a constant possibility, and misunderstandings are commonplace. Meanings are often obscure to the observer who can spend time studying recorded and transcribed texts. It is difficult to make out, for example, what is present to the minds of the speakers in this exchange.

Exchange type	Opening		Answering		Follow-up	
teaching elicit	Where's your Humpty Dumpty, sitting on a wall?	el.				
re-initiate	Is he all ready to fall off?	el.				
re-initiate	Is he a bit wobbly?	el.	I got *two* Humpty Dumpties!		Oh, you can't have *two* Humpty Dumpties! He has to	ev. com.

Exchange type	Opening		Answering		Follow-up	
					sit on a wall!	

The analysis comes nowhere near explaining the evident strangeness of the utterance. To do that, it is necessary to uncover contrasting presuppositions that underlie the (apparently) mismatched utterances. Some partial indications are available in terms of the observer's recollection, and would have been preserved if video tape had been available for the recording. The nursery rhyme was treated by this teacher as an action song. Her initial questions were designed to remind children of the appropriate actions, that is to clench one fist, to represent the egg, and to place the other with the thumb uppermost and the palm facing the body, to represent the wall on which Humpty is seated. This pupil seems to suppose that 'Humpty Dumpty' is here used as a synonym for 'hand', and (reasonably enough) declared that she had *two* of them. Alternatively she may have supposed that she could, if she liked, make two Humpties, and *no* wall. The teacher, faced with a whole class, was more concerned to get the actions imitated, and the song under way, than she was to sort out a misunderstanding that may have arisen from a lexical mistake, or may have had its origin in a failure to perceive the function of an utterance, accompanied by unfamiliarity with the actions to accompany the rhyme. She could not, however, altogether ignore such a patently odd utterance, and she countered it with what is at first hearing one even odder, though in its context her meaning is clear enough to the adult observer, and can be paraphrased like this: 'you can't have both fists clenched to represent eggs – you need one to represent the wall.' It is possible that the little girl may not have understood her teacher's explanation to mean anything except an instruction to be quiet and to do as she saw the others doing. If, however, her mistake was to suppose that she had the option of *not* making a wall, then the teacher's response was a useful one. Actions to accompany a song belong to the class of items that have to be learned and performed, and that offer no scope for individual choice.

Children repeatedly encounter experiences of this sort – experiences where adult use of language causes them to make reasonable, but wrong inferences, or where their understanding of the function of an utterance differs from the intention of the speaker, or where adults assume that children are in possession of a set of suppositions derived from knowledge that in fact they do not have. The limited conversational rights assigned to children do not include the right to take the sort of initiatives in classroom discourse that would be likely to lead to a rapid resolution of the resulting confusion. Pupils rarely say to teachers, 'What do you mean?' or 'What are we doing this for?', and if they do, the question is *heard* as challenging, even defiant, rather than as seriously enquiring. Efforts at a much later stage of the educational process to discourage in students an uncritical acceptance of authoritative pronouncements are disappointing in relation to the effort involved, and this is hardly a matter for surprise. Participation in well-formed discourse does not necessarily entail understanding.

None the less, misunderstanding arising from mismatch of experience was not always allowed to persist. Teachers were prepared to interrupt activity and to spend time on digression if they thought an evident misconception might cause alarm or upset to a child. This is what happens in the following series of exchanges, and illustrates the way in which, despite the pressure of many preoccupations, a teacher can utilise her control of the discourse in such a way as to resolve the misunderstandings that arise in the course of it. The setting is an early lesson using *Breakthrough to Literacy*, and the children were learning to associate the spoken and the written forms of the word 'house'. The topic prompted an initiating move on the part of one of the pupils:

We're going to live in a cottage and it won't be bricks!

The following exchange then took place:

Exchange type	Opening		Answering		Follow-up	
teaching elicit	Where will the straw be?	el.	On holiday.	rep.	No.	ev.
teaching elicit	Will the sides of the house be made of bricks?	el.				

Exchange type	Opening		Answering		Follow-up	
re-initiate	Have you seen your cottage?	el.	Not yet.	rep.	I think you'll find that only the *roof* is made of straw.	

Several misunderstandings are involved here, some (but not all) of which can be disentangled by the observer. The context was talk about houses and building materials, and it looks as if the initial contribution may mean that this child knows she is going to live in a stone-built house, or one having rendered surfaces. The teacher's assumption that she thought the cottage might be built of straw is explicable only if one knows (as I did) that on the previous day the teacher had told the children the story of the three little pigs, and had shown them the illustration in the book. She believed (rightly or not) that the tale was very much present in the children's minds. To a teacher, though not necessarily to a child who recollected the story of the preceding day, straw is a possible building material in the everyday world only if it is used as thatch. The expected, and so the 'right' answer to her question was therefore 'on the roof'. The child however seems to have interpreted her question to mean 'in what circumstances would you live in this house not made of bricks?', and answered the question 'on holiday'. The teacher's 'No' was intended, and the intonation made the intention quite apparent, to close that part of the interchange, and to discard it. She tried again, with another question that seemed to be the first of a sequence intended to get the answer she wanted initially. She succeeded only in producing a puzzled silence. So she tried a fresh tack: only the *roof* she said, will be made of straw. Any alarm the child may have felt at the prospect of a holiday spent in a cottage vulnerable to wolves and their huffing and puffing should be dismissed. There is no evidence in the text that such an anxiety had, in fact, crossed the pupil's mind. This is simply an instance of mismatch between the assumptions of adult and child of a kind so common, and when once the observer stops to examine it, so complicated, that it is not surprising that teachers rarely do so.

Misunderstandings like this arise where discourse is well-formed. Mistakes, on the part of the hearers, of the function of utterances intended by speakers, may compound misunderstandings but do not account for them. Nor can they be explained as the effect of inexperience on the teacher's part. Very experienced teachers are frequently involved in tangles of misconception, and the strategy that this teacher employs — of stopping the discourse and starting again with another question, supposedly easier to answer, is as likely to increase the confusion as it is to resolve it. Examples of non-comprehension, miscomprehension, and cross-purpose could be multiplied. They are part of the texture of the verbal interchange of classrooms. It is likely that in classrooms, and indeed in families, misunderstandings are less frequent as children grow older, partly because their experience more nearly coincides with that of adults about them, and partly because the diminishing inequality between participants in discourse makes it possible for mistakes to be repaired by either. It is certainly not the case that misunderstandings do not occur between adults who have equal conversational rights, or fewer difficulties than teachers and their young pupils experience in knowing what is, and what is not, shared knowledge. They patently do, and every sort of situated discourse has to make room for repair strategies. In the discourse of teachers and pupils they occur frequently. Teachers reinitiate eliciting moves, often more than once; loops may take the discourse back to an earlier stage and this makes for much of the redundancy which is sometimes noticed (and criticised) in the spoken interaction between adults and children. It has a function that seems indispensable. It is often observed, in addition, that there seems to be too little room for pupil talk, and that too many of the eliciting moves made by teachers allow of only a brief and stereotyped answer. A close look at the complicated mistakes that occur as a result of pupil initiatives, and a realistic consideration of the sort of difficulties entailed by a serious attempt on the part of teachers to resolve misunderstandings suggests a modification of such a view. Answers that involve guessing what is in the mind of the questioner and supplying it, do at least allow of untroubled progress of the kind that can be planned ahead. This is not in itself an answer to the criticism, virtually always implied if not stated, that such guesswork is a trivial activity. I do not deny that it is often allowed to persist too long, but in respect of the youngest pupils I suggest that it has a necessary function in narrowing by degrees the initially huge gap between the teacher's and the pupil's presuppositions and perceptions.

Learning to react to directives

From time to time it was observable that, contrary to teachers' habits of expectation, young pupils either disregarded or seemed to reject the responding role assigned to them, and the resulting disturbance to the smooth running of the classroom could neither be amended nor easily ignored. In these circumstances teachers can respond in only one of two ways: either the boy or girl in question does not know, and must be taught, what is expected, or he or she *does* know the rules, and is trying out the possibility of disregarding them. Teachers must make such judgments immediately, and in the face of all sorts of other demands on their attention. The necessity often arose from children's preference for activities of their own devising to any one of several from which they were required to choose. The following excerpt represents a very usual strategy for dealing with such a situation:

Pupil: (whispering to another) We'll play in the windows.
Pupil: Yes – go on.
Teacher: (to a third pupil) They're busy, aren't they? They're very
    busy. Look at Martin. (There is a perceptible rise in the level of
    noise.) Now don't be silly. No more nonsense. Oh, what's that
    you've got there?

Initially the teacher was simply exercising a general supervision. In their interaction with each other, children found it quite natural to take conversational initiatives and decisions about how they would like to spend their time. However, whispering children playing in classroom window bays partially obscured by large items of furniture, are bound to attract the attention of a careful teacher. They may very well be up to no good. It is by no means certain that they really are 'busy' in the classroom sense of absorbed in legitimate activity. The teacher's confident assertion that they *are* is not to be taken at its face value. There is a risk that they may interpret what she says as a positive evaluation of their activity. It is one she decides to take. The intention (clear to the observer from her intonation) is to signal to them that they have been identified and noticed, and to me (as the adult witness) that she is well aware of the possibility of misdemeanour, and had judged it best to do no more at the moment than to indicate to the whispering pair that they had better not push their luck. Any reference by a teacher to forbidden activity is meant to be interpreted as an instruction to desist from it. This is one of the situational rules for classroom

discourse identified by Sinclair and Coulthard (*TAD*, p. 30) and it
seems to be operative here. Initially the children did seem however to
take the teacher's apparent commendation at its face value. However,
only quiet misbehaviour allowed of such indirect, and as it appeared,
ambiguous handling. Noise met at once with an unmistakable direction
to stop, and the instruction was at once succeeded by a question, the
function of which seemed to be to distract attention from the forbidden activity and from the restriction placed on it.

A little later the same teacher discovered, in that part of the room
where easels were set up and painting equipment was available, a small
girl, standing by her easel, overall on, and brush in hand, but not
painting. She seemed to have lost interest in the activity, having hardly
begun. This was not uncommon, nor was the coaxing by which the
teacher tried to get her to continue:

Teacher: I'd be glad of some paintings for my wall. Wouldn't you do
some paintings for me Ruth? For my wall?

Here the school activity was presented, (as it is very often) as a task
performed in order to oblige a teacher. Since most children do very
much want to please their teacher, this is often a successful strategy. It
is not of course specific to the classroom; it is used by parents and by
adults generally in relation to children too young to appreciate that
some not especially welcome or attractive things have to be done in
everyone's interest, including their own. It can of course be argued
that children learn anyway that finding out what the teacher wants, and
doing it, constitutes the primary duty of a pupil, and that considered as
a learning strategy this is not a very good one, having no more than a
slight and quickly exhausted usefulness.

These were no more, however, than ripples on a usually smooth
surface. In the nursery, and in the reception class, a quietly spoken
firmness of manner was usually enough to secure compliance. However,
one of the teachers had to cope with a persistently disobedient little
boy. At 5, his behaviour seemed to challenge her authority. She was
under corresponding pressure to assert it. She succeeded too, at any
rate in the short term, though not, in the event, by verbal means. The
child in question, Chatinder, understood and spoke English very imper-
fectly, and I was puzzled to find his slight and inaccurate knowledge of
the sound system of English not recognised as a significant contribution
to the conflict of wills that developed from this sort of interchange:

Teacher: Right. What does that say?
   (no intelligible response. The teacher is evidently annoyed.)
Teacher: Chatinder. Chatinder.

Worse was to come. Instructions given by the teacher were ignored altogether. A long succession of directives got no reacting move.

Teacher: Put your legs down Chatinder. Don't make me cross.
   (Again there is an attempt at a reply, but it is not intelligible to
   teacher nor observer.)
Teacher: Read the story first love –
   'Two dads are going to the park.'
   You write it please.
   (There is no attempt to comply.)
   Don't get off that seat till you've written it.
   Are you listening? 'Cos I shall get cross if you are going to be silly.
   You're a big boy now please . . . .
   Show me what a big boy you can be.

The teacher here assumed that however limited Chatinder's English, there were enough clues available in the situation to enable him to understand the function of her utterances, and to comply minimally, at least, by desisting from fidgeting and worse, and making some show of doing what the others were doing. She expected him to learn that freedom of movement and a choice among several activities, the norms of her classroom, were privileges he could forfeit, and that with them he risked losing her approval and his new status of a 'big boy'. He was one of only two pupils in that classroom not of English parentage. The other was the child of a mother whose fluency in several languages included a near-native control of English. He had been brought up to speak English as his first language, and it may be that his effortless fluency did Chatinder an unwitting disservice. Unlike the children whose situation was described in chapter 3, Chatinder was isolated by his incomprehension of the language spoken everywhere about him. His teacher's warnings, however, were either deliberately disregarded or were simply not understood. Chatinder would not stay in one place, engaged in a single activity, for even a limited time. He rushed about the classroom, upsetting other children, damaging toys, and endangering equipment, and found himself encountering the anger of his teacher and a set of instructions directly and unmistakably expressed and sharply delivered:

Teacher: Chatinder, sit down! Sit down. Put your book on the table.
Now listen. If you're naughty again, I shall have to smack you.
Do you like being smacked? Well, you'd better stop then, or you'll
get it. Come on. Do your writing. All the other children have done
some writing, and you're as clever as they are, aren't you?

The last thing this teacher wanted to do in fact was to smack Chatinder,
though she invoked an obligation to do so if he failed to respond to
persuasion. (That compulsion seemed to the observer real enough. No
teacher could have tolerated the degree of disturbance Chatinder was
causing.) Chatinder seemed impervious to warnings, threats, and coaxing, and quite unresponsive to the idea that most children seemed
already to understand, namely that there was competition in the classroom for approval and success, into which everyone entered. Chatinder
seemed by contrast uncomprehending of that part of the role of pupil,
or unwilling to undertake it, and in the absence of a language in common
it was hardly possible to determine which of the two made the greater
contribution to his unacceptable behaviour. No interpreter was to be
had. His misbehaviour was perceived rather as that of a child too young
to have acquired language than as that of one who did not understand
English. Within a day or two of arrival he was identified as a problem —
a source of disruption and an occasion of anxiety to his teacher, who
was very willing to discuss the strategies which, in the initial weeks of
the term, she employed.

As soon as she found he made no coherent response to anything she
said to him, she resorted to picking him up and holding him close, treating him, as she said, just as she would a baby or a toddler, so as to
ensure that he experienced restraint, while at the same time he was
assured that restraint in no way entailed rejection. In this way was
acted out the warning already given — that only conformity would
secure and retain his 'big boy' status, and in this way his teacher gained
the upper hand without relinquishing her professional stance of kindly
and benevolent control.

It seems beyond dispute that teachers start with a thoroughly internalised set of expectations about the interaction in classrooms and the
role relations that the interaction reflects and reinforces. These expectations are not as a rule verbalised, and, in a sense, they do not need to be.
Challenges like that presented by Chatinder, for whom his teacher's
expectations seemed no more than partially accessible are unfamiliar to
many teachers, and, in any case, did not occur very often. Teachers are
adult, confident, and in the classroom they occupy their own ground.

In relation to these young children, the sort of physical restraint Chatinder's teacher exercised is practicable and acceptable. Children aged 5 can usually be lifted or carried out of danger or mischief if they persist in disregarding adult directions. Where the dominant, responsible role of the teacher is resisted and defied by young children, their resistance is perceived as a source of perfectly legitimate annoyance, warranting firm action, but certainly not as a serious threat.

For practical purposes it may not be necessary that teachers should verbalise the expectations they have of their pupils, but the consequence of their not doing so is that these are, and in general remain, inaccessible to processes of appraisal and consequent modification. Newcomers to the educational system do not get, as the naive observer might suppose they would, a fresh start. Rather, they are cast for parts already established in innumerable rehearsals. If this is generally true, it goes some way to account for what has often been observed, the conservatism that is apparent in education, and that coexists with serious, persistent, and well-publicised innovation. It directs attention to two questions, one generally interesting, and one of particular concern to anyone interested in the discourse of the classroom. The first is where do teachers get their expectations about what is suitable, proper, and indeed inevitable, from? The second is this: does the nature of the process of learning and teaching determine the structure of the texts that teachers and pupils create in classrooms?

So far as the first question is concerned, my experience of the professional preparation of teachers leads me to think that these expectations are not created by the process of institutionalised training. Conversely, institutions embody, and confirm in their students, society's expectations about what teachers do, and what roles they assume in relation to pupils at different stages of their education. Students start training to be teachers having had more than a decade of exposure to the educational system of this country, and continue as they have begun, unaware that different assumptions from those embodied in it are possible. Lacking the means of detachment from these, they are locked in as securely as were those English-speaking American teachers of Amerindian pupils as studied by Philips (1972). They were dismayed and then exasperated at not getting answering in response to their initiating moves. There was no follow-up to offer, no encouragement for their pupils, and no acknowledgment of their own efforts. They perceived the absence of answering moves as critical, hostile, even defiant. To the Amerindian pupil learning is a private activity, and practice is a solitary one. Clumsy and inept actions are not to be exposed to the general view, and only when practice has made perfect is newly acquired skill ready to be displayed. Ours is a culture that perceives answering moves as proper to the learner role, the necessary if not the sufficient condition of learning, the indispensable evidence of it. Private and solitary concentration is a learning strategy belonging to other places in the educational system, and to more advanced learners.

The discourse that the Birmingham work describes, and to which, I have argued, very young learners assimilate, in general, rapidly and readily, clearly makes possible a strategy for teaching and learning. It is characteristic of such discourse that choice, and responsibility, belong to the adult. Decisions about the topic, about the pace, about starting and stopping, digression and return, are the teacher's, and leave few decisions that can be taken by the learner. Pupils take, relative to the teacher, few initiatives, and these are taken with the teacher's consent, and, as a rule, at her prompting. Having few options, pupils have also few responsibilities. Nobody but the teacher has an obligation to keep the discourse in being, and only the teacher is held responsible if, for whatever reason, its coherence breaks down altogether. Pupils may lapse into a non-participating silence. The teacher has no such option, but she has almost every other privilege. Only she evaluates what the pupils offer in response, and the crucial decision, the decision about what constitutes relevance to the matter in hand, is for her alone. It is almost impossible for a pupil to ask a question about the relevance of items to each other, or about the evidence for a claim, or about what would be the prerequisites of understanding a particular matter, without seeming to challenge very directly the teacher's personal authority. The very word docile, meaning teachable, suggests passivity. A responding, uncritical participant *is* teachable. It is a learning strategy well adapted to cope with the assimilation of kinds of knowledge that do not require to be subjected to processes of selection or criticism in the process of transmission. Everyone, it is generally assumed, needs to acquire some information of this sort, though the questions how much, and when, and of what kind, do not admit of ready answers. What *is* questionable is whether such learning, and the strategy appropriate to it, need predominate to the extent that it does. The idea of learning as a process by which the culture is transmitted, essentially unchanged, from one generation to the next is currently unfashionable and deserves more serious examination than it usually receives, but is, at best, of no more than limited application. If this is so, then pupils need not so much a single, generally dominant learning strategy, but a repertoire of strategies increasing in number and in flexibility of

application, with the increasing variety and difficulty of the things they
need to learn. Recent work that emphasises the need for small groups
of learners to engage in purposeful talk moves in this direction. So does
the increased willingness of teachers (relative to the past) to allow
children to have their often rather hesitant say, and to avoid cutting
them short. This was the point at which to pursue the question whether
the learning and teaching processes, as these are understood in our
classrooms and our culture, determine the structure of the discourse.
The question invited enquiry. Were the constraints as difficult to avoid
as they seemed to be?

Testing the feasibility of another sort of didactic discourse

As a participant observer in the classroom I was able to play the teacher's
role from time to time, and I did so in relation to one small boy, a
newcomer to the reception class, whom I noticed engaged in a task he
found decidedly taxing. I set myself to find out whether it was possible
to get him to verbalise his way to a solution, without either creating
typically didactic text, and without studious and self-conscious avoidance of it. It seems to me that he and I did create text that was unusual
in interesting ways, and that an analysis of it, in terms of the Birmingham
(Sinclair and Coulthard, 1975) model, indicates some of the ways in
which it was unusual.

The circumstances were these. Gerard was using a dotted line, provided by his teacher, as he traced with a pencil the letters of his own
name. I sat down beside him so that I could observe what he did without getting in his way. The left-right direction was evidently unfamiliar.
The letter shapes required concentration. He had some trouble grasping
and manipulating the pencil. Initially he made the mistake of starting
with the pencil in the middle of the dotted guide, and moving towards
the left, and in my role of teacher I recalled his attention to the left-
right direction of English writing:

Teacher: Now the next one . . . going the wrong way Gerard. You
    want to go that way when you write.
Gerard: There!

Once he had understood the change, and made it, Gerard evaluated his
own work, with a satisfied 'There!', and at once sought advice for the
next stage of the task.

Gerard: What do you do a straight?
Teacher: Well, I should do a curve, a curve first like *that*, and then a
    straight across there.

At that point, the teacher did more than simply respond to Gerard's
question. She went on to give instructions and draw Gerard's attention
to a mistake. He was quick to recognise that a mistake *had* been made,
and he announced what he intended to do to put it right. His teacher
just acknowledged and confirmed his decision.

Teacher: Would you like to go over it? . . . Good. Now the next one
    . . . you've left one out look. You've written those two and left
    one out.
Gerard: I'll do it in that space there.
Teacher: I think you could.

Once the amendment had been made, it was Gerard, not the teacher,
who signalled the start of a fresh topic (another *transaction* in
Birmingham terms) and followed it by other questions:

Gerard: Now. I'll do a circle first, don't you?
Teacher: Yes.
Gerard: And then a circle at the bottom?
Teacher: That's the way.

The initiating moves were Gerard's; the confirmatory responses were his
teacher's. This is not well-formed classroom discourse, but it is hard to
contest the intuitive judgment that learning was actually happening. He
seemed at this stage to need some direction, and with this assistance,
the task was rapidly concluded:

Teacher: Well actually you need the circle *this* side of the straight . . .
    well perhaps you'd like to put another one under . . . d'you see
    the difference? Now make it a little bit taller . . . taller than that
    . . . wants to come up here look, like this . . . you follow with the
    dots now and you'll soon see. Well done Gerard. Can you write
    anything else beside your name?

A series of initiating moves, this time by his teacher, directive in their
function, were rapidly and silently followed by reacting moves by
Gerard. At the conclusion there was feedback — a positive evaluation

by the teacher. Teacher and pupil slipped into a series of teaching exchanges — and then out again, for the teacher's attempts to extend the task further met with a polite, but decided 'no'. The decision that the job was complete, and that no more was to be done at that present time, was Gerard's. The interaction was unusual in several respects, and these crucial ones. Teacher and learner each made initiating and responding moves. Gerard evaluated his own performance, he signalled when a fresh start was needed, he decided when the transaction was finished. All these are decisions that typically pupils do not make, and are in general supposed too inexperienced to be capable of making. It is not the case, however, that there is here a simple exchange of roles between teacher and taught. No play-acting was involved, and the teacher's directions and information and reassurance were essential to the successful completion of the task in hand. It may of course be objected that this passage of interaction was possible only because I was not responsible for the activities of all the children in the room. This was of course true, but it should be added that the room was large, and that responsibility was normally shared by at least two people. Additional adults were present for at least part of the session. In giving a few minutes' concentrated attention to a single pupil I was doing nothing that was in any way unusual, and mine was only a privileged position to the extent that I was not accountable (as a teacher must be, but as other adults in the classroom were not) for the welfare and safety of everyone in the class.

In these few minutes, discourse having unusual structure, in part well-formed by the standards and in the way already discussed, and in part deviant from the standards was, I believe, a vehicle of effective learning. Gerard was at the end, more secure in his recognition of the left-right direction of English writing than he had been at the start. He had learned that complicated letter shapes can be resolved into simpler ones. He was a measurable step nearer to literacy. He brought to the task, apparently, a readiness to recognise mistakes without feeling either humiliated or baffled. He saw his teacher as someone in possession of relevant experience and of interest and good will in relation to him, and he treated both as a resource at his disposal. He had some control over the pace of the activity and over its duration. From the beginning the successful outcome of the undertaking was important to him, and adult encouragement, though probably welcome, appeared no more than secondary and incidental. He assumed some of the functions that are as a rule the exclusive privileges of the teacher, and by doing so he became an effective and resourceful learner.

At advanced stages of the educational process it is generally accepted that learning will be largely self-motivated, that the teacher's role will increasingly be that of adviser, and that at least the abler and more successful learners will identify what they want and need to study. There is a general, though as a rule an unexamined assumption, that in the process of schooling pupils advance from a stage where, typically, they can manage no more than brief and controlled responses to teachers' initiatives, and depend heavily on teachers' evaluation to sustain their willingness to continue, to a late stage where they assume some responsibility and exercise a significant degree of choice. It is assumed too that while it is very regrettable that no more than a minority actually achieve any degree of freedom and independence, it is inevitable this should be so. The implication is that maturity, experience, and an unusual endowment of intelligence are prerequisites of independent, self-motivated learning. An examination of the text I have quoted above suggests that the prerequisites may in fact be quite different. Gerard was not at all experienced in terms of institutionalised learning. At nearly five, he was not yet securely in control of some parts of the grammar of English, but he was very well able to use it for purposes of interpersonal communication and as a means of finding out what he needed to know. For him the interpersonal and the heuristic functions of language, to use Halliday's terms, were well developed. The learning task, rudimentary in adult judgment, had meaning and importance for him. Although it had initially been proposed by his class teacher, he had made her purposes very much his own. There is no sign that he regarded it as imposed from outside, or that he wanted to dispose of it with minimal expenditure of effort and time. His readiness to risk being wrong, to seek and use assistance, his satisfaction at its completion, must stem from his recognition of the meaning of the task for him.

Nobody doubts that effective learning is contingent on pupils' ability to perceive meaning in the fine detail of the educational process. Teachers readily acknowledge the difficulty of avoiding the setting of tasks that mean nothing to those who have to do them. When this is so, it is difficult to suppose that any motivation is available other than the seeking and enjoyment of approval, or that there can be any reason for them to seek out assistance or to determine the pace at which they will proceed. The teacher is then obliged to take on a permanent occupation of the dominant role, and to take virtually all the initiatives. The acceptance of such an obligation assumes, and perpetuates, an active organising function confined to the teacher, and an acquiescent response for the learner. This is a view persuasively argued by Burton (1976) who arrives at it by a rather different route. She contrasts two sets of materials designed for older children than these, at the lower end of the primary age range. Each set is designed to assist in language development. The materials by Schiach (1972), *Teach them to Speak* assumes in ordinary children a degree of ignorance and ineptitude in the use of their mother tongue that is simply implausible in the face of unprejudiced observation. The other is the material prepared by Wight and his associates, with the needs of multi-ethnic urban primary schools in mind, and entitled *Concept 7/9*. It provides a variety of game-like activities that supposes that the users already have considerable knowledge of English and its uses, and seeks to extend that knowledge to include experiences like classification and inference that are particularly necessary to effective learning. *Concept 7/9*, unlike the material with which it is contrasted, has few successors, and its attribution to quite young children of control over a variety of language functions, while it has been often demonstrated, still does not meet with widespread acceptance.

Some tentative conclusions

It began to look as if it was not so much the teaching and learning processes that determined the structure of classroom text so much as the many-to-one relations that children are obliged to accept on entry to school. Becoming a pupil entails becoming one of a group of children at about the same age. The natural hierarchy of older and younger no longer obtains. Turns have to be taken. Nobody can claim more than a share of the available toys and materials and adult attention, and further, these things have to be competed for, and the competition is regulated. Classroom discourse, that typically secures for the teacher a dominant role only briefly and at her own initiative relaxed, makes possible for her the discharge of a primary obligation often overlooked in discussions about education, the obligation to control a number of pupils so as to ensure the safety of each of them. The structure of the discourse reflects the classroom social structure, and learning to be a pupil involves learning to participate in the expected ways, in both. In so far as it imposes on the pupil, most of the time, passivity and brevity, it does not commend itself as more than a limited and inflexible medium for learning. It is a fact of our society, culturally transmitted and rapidly assimilated, owing little to institutionalised and explicit forms of professional training, and deriving from a teacher's custodial rather than from her educative function.

This was an interim conviction. Obviously I should want to return to some discussion of the relation between the structure of discourse, the perceptions of teachers, and the learning done by pupils. The immediate next step was to attend to individual learning of the discourse rules, and if possible to take some account of the likelihood that the text I had been able to observe and record, while generally well formed and analysable, might be the product of a class in reciprocal relation to a teacher that included individuals learning at different rates and in different ways. The satisfactorily responsive class might indeed include some bewildered, silent, or randomly answering children. At this stage I needed a different tool for investigation than the participant observation I had employed so far. A mode of approach was required that would allow me to elicit from children what they knew and could do, from the shy and the talkative alike, and to attend carefully to those naturally taciturn children who are underrepresented by observer and record alike. I needed to be in a position to select a sample of children which, while its size would be limited by the limited resources at my disposal, would be representative, and would be in principle extendable.

The help of children
at a Midland primary school,
of their teacher
and of their head teacher
is gratefully acknowledged.

Mary Willes

Let's make a story about school!

Author: _____

Age: _____

Date: _____

School: _____

One part of their classroom was made to look like a real house. Sometimes the children did real cooking. In this picture though, they have just given Miss Smith a pretend cup of tea.

What do you think she said?

On that morning, Miss Smith took some of the children into the reading corner. Here they are, learning to read. Miss Smith is holding up a card, and on the card is the word she wants them to notice and remember. If you were as close to Miss Smith as the children are, you would see that the card looks like this—

$$\boxed{\text{d o g}}$$

It says 'dog'. What do you think Miss Smith is saying?
And what do you think happens then?

Then Miss Smith shows them the cards again, but this time she hopes that everyone will remember them. She held up the card that said

$$\boxed{\text{t o y}}$$

again, and what do you think she said?
Tony, that's this boy, remembered all right, so what do you think he said?
What do you think Miss Smith said then?

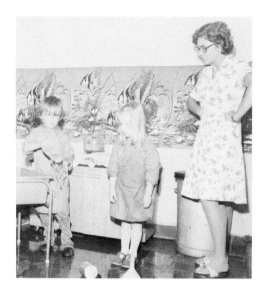

Just then Miss Smith noticed one of the boys—you can see him in the picture, his name is Jim . . .
I wonder if you can see what Miss Smith noticed?
'Jim,' she said, 'I do believe you've filled your *shoe* with water!'
What do you think happened then?

She looked at the floor where the children had been measuring out water.
Miss Smith said 'There's a big puddle of water on the floor. And just inside the cupboard there's a mop and bucket.'
What do you think happened then?

By this time everyone felt quite sure about all the words, so when Miss Smith held up again the card that said

| d o g |

they *all* called out—well, what do you think they all called out?
Do you think Miss Smith was pleased?
What do you think she said?

It was nearly time for them to stop and to do something different. In the picture you can see Miss Smith holding up the clock face she uses to teach the children how to tell the time. She has moved the hands to ten o'clock. What do you think she is saying?

7

Pupils' views of the interactional experience of the classroom

The evidence of make-believe play

When I began work in the nursery and reception classes I discussed with teachers the possibility that I might be well placed to observe children playing at schools, and that such observation would allow of insight into those children's perceptions of what teachers and their classes typically do, what they say, and how they respond. Teachers encouraged me to be on the alert for play of this sort; it was not at all uncommon — and I would find, they assured me, that in the context of such make-believe, teachers were regularly represented as old-fashioned, authoritarian figures. In fact I observed no play at all of this sort for some considerable time. Of course this does not mean it did not occur at all, but it certainly did not occur constantly and regularly. I had no evidence, among the children I worked with, of any compelling wish to enact a representation of their experience. Make-believe play of other kinds they engaged in every day. They played at buses, at mothers and fathers, at variations of cops and robbers, at hospitals. The detail of their make-believe was heavily dependent on the provision of toys and equipment that suggested particular activities and places. The Wendy house, with its range of scaled-down furnishings and equipment, was standard provision, and it was regularly the scene of make-believe family life. Where a toy steering wheel and gearbox were at hand, together with a ticket collector's punch and peaked cap, a game of buses was a regular favourite. In general terms, however, the make-believe I observed among the youngest children was neither so spontaneous, nor so inventive as I had expected. It was not the case that the youngest children relied on language for the creation of imagined settings and circumstances, and pressed into the service of imagination whatever objects were available. Their games shifted, with dreamlike suddenness, from one set of imagined circumstances to another. I had

149

the sense of watching the imaginative function of language among these 4-year olds at an early and undeveloped stage, where it was possible for them to indicate, but not to sustain or to develop, a fiction. What Luria and Yudovich (1968) observed of the delayed language development of the 5-year-old twins they studied applied aptly to these normally developing but younger children; they seemed

> unable to detach the word from the action, to master orienting, planning activity, to formulate the aims of the activity with the aid of speech, and so to subordinate their further activity to this verbal formulation. (p. 121)

Given that children in nursery classes had little wish to represent to themselves the situation of the classroom, those a year older, in the first year of full-time compulsory schooling, might do so. If 'schools' was an occasional rather than a regular game, and much time might elapse without opportunity of observing it, then perhaps the children might be persuaded by the same means as had so effectively promoted play at buses, that is to say by the provision of appropriate toys? There would be some loss of spontaneity, but not a total loss.

With this possibility in mind I sought and obtained permission to introduce in a classroom of 5-year-olds already very well supplied with all sorts of play equipment, a new item, a Fisher Price Playschool, designed by the manufacturers for children between the ages of 3 and 6. (Reeder made use of it in his 1975 study.) It was immediately liked, and the chance to play with it was regarded as a treat. The toy represents an old-fashioned rural school, having only one room, a steeply pitched roof, and a school bell. It opens up to reveal four small dolls and a teacher doll. These can be moved from their desks to sit securely in the swings and roundabout outside in the playground. There is a blackboard and chalks, and figures and letters that magically adhere to the magnet board. These are deliberately out of scale with the model, large enough to invite the user to identify with the teacher doll, who is distinguished from the rest by her hair drawn back in a bun, and her superior desk, complete with open register and apple. Groups of children were offered, and eagerly took, the opportunity of playing with this toy. Most of the time was spent in handling the various attractively coloured pieces. For most of the children recognition that this was a 'school' with 'teacher' and 'pupils' occasioned no difficulty, but they did not imaginatively identify with what was represented. This was not always the case, however. One child, Tina, at once assumed the teacher role. She did so decisively, but not aggressively. In a tone of voice that was very confident and a good deal louder than usual, she took on one of the teacher's most readily imitable functions, and I was able to record, and later to transcribe, the following:

Tina: I'm taking register now! David!
David: Yes Miss Brown.

David was left in no doubt what he had to do. Tina evidently understood both parts of the routine:

Tina: You'll have to say the names for 'em. You'll have to say 'Yes Miss Brown' too. David.
David: Yes Miss Brown.

A little later this dialogue was repeated, but with an extension:

Tina: Who's staying dinners? — done the register. *You're* staying dinners. (She rings the bell) *That* means it's dinner time.
David: It isn't!

These 5-year-olds were aware of how the routine of registration works, and of the teacher as somebody in authority, who makes decisions, organises the day, and expects other people to conform. Except in his last, exasperated utterance, David adopted a prompt, compliant manner and spoke more briefly and quietly than Tina did.

Playing the part of an *effective* teacher, that is, of someone who provides information at the same time new and appropriate, one whose directives and elicitations facilitate and test learning, requires knowledge and experience that 5-year-olds simply do not have. Clearly a great deal of caution is required in drawing inferences from the evidence of make-believe play about children's perceptions of what it is to be a teacher, but it does usefully supplement what can be learned from other sources. Such evidence as I was able to obtain, from observation and from talking to teachers, suggests that of the welter of new experience that confronts the newcomer to school, it is the distinctive organisational routines that have for him vitality and importance, and the control of these routines constitutes for him the authority of the teacher. If this is so, it is of interest, and it deserves to be further explored. However, it affords little indication of a solution to the questions that were central to my concern. I wanted to know how

children perceived the relations of teacher and taught, and the rules
that obtain in the spoken interaction of the classroom. It was very
evident that in observing what spontaneously occurred, and in observing what happened when I set up deliberately situations that would
elicit what I wanted to observe, I could only expect, at best, to tap the
perceptions of those children who are naturally confident and talkative.
Participant observation is inevitably attracted to those whose responses
are easy to notice, record and study. They are, as a rule, a minority. At
this point I needed to devise some means of eliciting and comparing the
perceptions of a representative sample of children. Observation needed
to be extended by some means of eliciting from the children what, and
how much, they understood.

Towards a design for an empirical study

In working on a means of doing this there were some assumptions that,
on the basis of the earlier work, I felt I could make. A child, learning to
be a pupil, can rely on his teacher to make nearly all the initiating
moves. Questions asked by pupils, informative observations made by
them are not excluded, they can contribute to well-formed discourse.
They are however relatively rare. A pupil has the option of making the
initiating move, but, unlike his teacher, he has the option of *not* doing
so. He must however, if he is to be a participant in what goes on, and
not just a presence in the room, understand the function of the initiating move his teacher makes, and, on the basis of that understanding, he
has to be able to predict from moment to moment what is going to
happen next. This is the basis of his developing understanding that, just
as he has some rights and obligations, so have others, that turns have to
be taken, that he must pay attention and expect a share (and no more)
of attention, and that the teacher, not he, and not anyone else, decides
who talks and when. I needed a device that would enable me to offer
each of a sample of children the chance to show me if they could, on
the basis of the different things teachers say, predict what would be
said or done next, and on the basis of the things pupils say and do,
predict the way in which a teacher is likely to respond. I needed some
control over the circumstances of their predictions. It could of course
be no more than a partial control, since there is no way of ensuring that
any two subjects (child or adult) perceive and interpret circumstances
in identical ways. None the less, I wanted to be in a position to make
qualified comparisons between children of the same chronological age,

between children of different ages, and between the responses made by the same child at different stages of his school experience. I set myself to design materials which would serve some of the purposes of a questionnaire in eliciting what I needed to know and could not expect to discover by other means, that would be appropriate and comprehensible in use with very young subjects, that would make selective use of the categories developed by the Birmingham team, and that would be in principle useable with a larger sample than the rather limited one with which, given the limited resources at my disposal, I would have to be content.

The materials I designed and used elicit what children know in something like the way that make-believe play elicits (from those who are willing to engage in it and can be observed doing so) what they know about classroom discourse. I put together an illustrated storybook, as much like those commonly used in classrooms for the youngest children as my limited resources would allow. I sought, and got, permission to have taken a series of illustrative photographs which I hoped children would recognise as representations of people and places very like themselves. In two respects the storybook differs from any of those from which, very frequently and regularly, teachers of the youngest children read aloud. It is, firstly, a story about entirely ordinary happenings — about a morning on a school day. Creative activities are followed by a reading lesson. The worst mishap occurs when one boy fills his shoe with water. It was always possible to point to an attractive display of books in any one of the classrooms where I worked, and to say truthfully that not one had so ordinary and familiar a setting. Secondly, the story is incomplete. Important parts of it have still to be written, and it is these which each child provides, working with the adult observer, who writes the child's contribution into a book which, once these have been transferred on to prepared sheets (so as to make study and comparison possible), becomes the child's own. My intention was to extend the cloze procedure which is so familiar a tool for language testing, to the area of discourse. In order to complete the story, an individual child has to be able to predict that initiating moves made by teachers will be followed by responding moves made by pupils, that different responses to different initiating moves are predictable; that answering moves are followed by feedback from teachers. He needs to know what realisations such moves typically have. I offered several opportunities for a realisation of each of the moves. Some of them are designed to discover whether the child understands that the situation described in words and pictures has to be taken into account in anticipating what would be said. There were deliberate limits to what was required. I did not try to devise a means of discovering whether newcomers to school recognise the boundaries of larger units of discourse, the *transaction* and the *lesson*, since it seemed to me that all that a young pupil needs to know about these, in order to participate fully in the work of the class, is that the choice of what is done and when, and the right to decide on changes of topic and of direction, belong to the teacher. The exercise had in addition to be kept within a young child's attention span. Even if, as I hoped, completing the story was regarded as an enjoyable activity, fifteen to twenty minutes was the upper limit of time I could expect to devote to it. I made some initial assumptions that were not borne out by every child in my sample; that the children would participate willingly in a game of my devising, not theirs, and that they would recognise that a story about ordinary people in familiar settings should sound plausible. In the event, few children seemed puzzled by the activity, and none was upset by it. Nearly all of them took the activity seriously and cheerfully, as just one more school task, and tried hard to complete the story properly. They were pleased at having so large a share of uninterrupted adult attention, and at having a tangible reward for their efforts. Though my limited resources would not allow of a large sample, I hoped that the sample would be in principle capable of extension, would be representative, and would include a wide range of children, from the confident ones whose class-room activity is easy to observe, study, and record, to the timid and retiring, who rarely participate in spontaneously occurring classroom discourse without deliberate persuasion by their teacher. Observation had suggested that experience of schooling, rather than chronological age, determines ability to participate, and that children differ in the rate at which they learn to comprehend to a degree not at all easily apparent to the teacher or to the observer. I saw these as suppositions needing to be established before other questions are examined relating to children who are, at the same time as they learn to be pupils, obliged to learn to be bilingual; this part of the study was confined to native speakers of British varieties of English.

What was not apparent to the children, and needs to be apparent only to the person who intends to use and to interpret the materials, is that they derive directly from the Birmingham model of classroom discourse, and for that reason the story is organised in three sections which need not, and do not, coincide with divisions in the narrative. The first section, the *Preliminaries*, requires the child to draw on what most children understand at entry to school, the alternating character of conversation, in all sorts of domestic and street settings outside the classroom. The purpose of this initial warm-up is to establish the subject in his role (almost certainly an unfamiliar one) of somebody whose responses are sought, receive close attention, and are written down. The second section is a sequence of exchanges in the sort of lesson that precedes reading for most children, when the recognition of word shapes is being taught. The text derives from observation of many lessons of this sort but it is fiction, simpler than reality, freer of asides, digressions, and changes of plan, and for these reasons probably more readily predictable than is often the case in reality. It is a long series of exchanges, and I would excuse its dullness, considered as fiction, on the grounds that the ability to understand what teachers say in such circumstances, to comprehend the function of her initiating moves, to predict what is intended to happen next, is central to the ability to function as a pupil. I wanted to offer repeated opportunities for children to show me that in a story, at a remove from reality, they understood that this was so. The third part of the story requires for its satisfactory completion the recognition that in some circumstances, but not in others, what are grammatically interrogatives may have a directive function. There is also a chance to show understanding of the *bidding* routine. A series of small-scale pilot studies suggested that this sort of cloze procedure disguised as a school task was not experienced as confusing or upsetting to the youngest children; that it discriminated quite sharply between those with longer and those with less experience of schooling, and that it could readily be used by other observers, who had had no part in its design.

The sample

My intention was to try the materials in use with a representative sample of children entering full-time schooling on the first day of the autumn term. The size of the sample was restricted by my estimate of the number I could expect to see in the first three weeks of that term (after which the term 'newcomer' could hardly be said to apply) and again at intervals during the first year of schooling. My decision not to include children of Asian or West Indian parentage in this part of the study was based on those earlier studies that confirmed the belief that learning to participate in classroom discourse in a language not your own, or in a variety of English very dissimilar from your own, is so different a matter as to require a different approach altogether. Within these restrictions, I selected every ninth school from an alphabetically ordered list of schools in a metropolitan borough. The total number of new entrants available did not then exceed the number I could expect to interview. The total sample comprised 42 pupils (24 boys and 18 girls). All were 5 or rising 5, born between August and March of the ensuing year. In addition I had a small control group of 8 children who on the same day entered the junior stage of their education, with two years of the infant school already accomplished. The children I saw first had spent 4 days (8 sessions) in school: those I saw last had had 12 days (24 sessions). Almost none of them could confidently be described as having had no previous experience at all of play group or nursery schooling. I was not able to obtain information about the extent of their experience, whether it was continuous or (as seemed often to have been the case) intermittent, or what sort of experience anticipatory of compulsory schooling it had provided.

In the April following the initial series of visits, when the children had been in school for seven months, I made a second visit. Of course I considered carefully the likelihood of their recalling the first occasion, and simply repeating the responses they had given me then. The alternative — the production of a second story book, at identical, or nearly identical level of difficulty, presented such an intractable problem that I resolved at least to see whether the children retained any distinct recollection of the first occasion, and were producing rehearsed answers. In the event they seemed simply not to remember the materials; some of them had no recollection of ever having seen me before. I decided to use the same materials on a second occasion, and counted myself fortunate to see 38 of the original sample of 42. A third visit was made weeks, rather than months, later to a subgroup, and this was differently organised and differently recorded.

On each of the September and April visits, I recorded the children's responses on a grid, having their names on the vertical axis, and, on the horizontal axis, abbreviated versions of those elements of the story which required completion by a response. Completing the grids was a time-consuming task, but (apart from the fact that it was one which ensured a careful examination of each entry irrespective of whether it was evidently interesting) the advantages were substantial. The user can shift attention easily from the total production of any one child on each occasion, to the responses produced by the whole sample to each one. The inclusion of a control group of older children allowed me to start making some comparisons during the interval that had to elapse between the first and the second series of visits.

As I began to examine and compare, my concern was divided between the children's production and the means I had employed to elicit it. Would the results of the preliminary trials, which suggested that the procedure discriminated well between children with more and with less experience of school, be borne out? If it discriminated between age groups would it discriminate within an age group? I was looking for evidence of a range of understanding among children near enough in age to be treated as a class. I had an additional problem, since the process of examination had of necessity to be extended over a period of some months, in securing consistency of evaluation — one that would be critical if the results of what could be no more than a feasibility study in terms of its scale, seemed, in the outcome, to warrant more extended use. In answer to this last problem, I set out a schedule in which I inserted against each cue (assigned a letter and a number for ease of reference) the expected *act*, or *move*, the one that was natural from someone familiar with classroom interaction. The actual realisation of that act or move was of course expected to vary. My intention here was not to set a series of targets for children, but rather to make explicit expectations which I could not avoid, and to check the consistency of those expectations.

The results of the first series of visits

Of the initial sample of 42 newcomers to full-time schooling, only four seemed at a loss to know what was required. As it happened, those four included the youngest and the oldest child in the sample. Given so narrow a span of ages, this is perhaps not especially remarkable, though. Those four children who provided no answer at all to many of the cues (and by 'many' is meant here 35 or more out of a possible 45) had already, within days of the start of term, been identified by their teachers as particularly unresponsive. This I interpreted as evidence that the cloze procedure, based on a fiction, was identifying something that corresponded to teachers' perceptions of children's actual classroom behaviour. One boy, who completed the story without particular difficulty, found the task too long and complained of boredom. Otherwise the children seemed neither surprised nor uneasy, and they seemed to understand what was wanted even if they could not comply with it. Some of them demonstrated an understanding that I found surprising in children not yet literate. Having given me the response they thought appropriate, they then repeated it, at a considerable dictation speed,

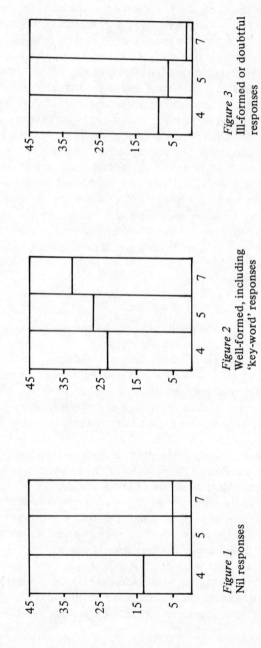

Figure 1
Nil responses

Figure 2
Well-formed, including
'key-word' responses

Figure 3
Ill-formed or doubtful
responses

These represent mean scores out of a total of 45 possible contexts, expressed to the nearest whole number

while I wrote it down. Most of them clearly enjoyed the collaborative nature, as they saw it, of the task. The 7-year-olds found it easy, though it was not the case, as my experience with the preliminary trials mistakenly led me to suppose, that they produced consistently and effortlessly well-formed responses. The block graphs (Figures 1, 2 and 3) make clear the contrast between 4-year-olds and 7-year-olds on the quantitative measures that derived from the procedure I have described. How to interpret the difference is not so clear, and has to be undertaken with caution. Where a child offers no response in answer to a cue it may mean just that he is nonplussed. He simply is not able to predict what would happen in the circumstances he is asked to envisage. This is a simplification that leaves out of account shyness, or inattention, or a habit of silence in the face of adult requests.

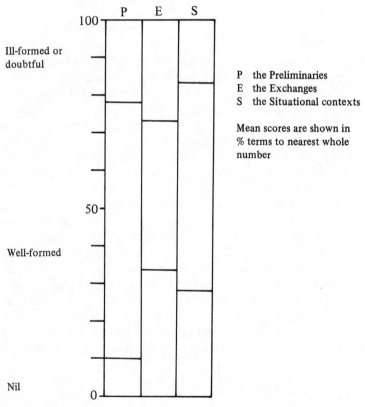

P   the Preliminaries
E   the Exchanges
S   the Situational contexts

Mean scores are shown in % terms to nearest whole number

Figure 4 The relative difficulty of different parts of the task for the 4-year-olds

Within the story-telling task I had tried to include different degrees of difficulty (Figure 4). My expectation was that the first set, the 'Preliminaries', would present few difficulties, even to the youngest children, since they were designed to be answered on the basis of familiarity with ordinary interchange of thanks and of greeting. I hoped for a successful, and in that respect reassuring introduction to the task. Asked, for instance, what the little girl shown tucking dolls into bed was saying to them, most of the children unhesitatingly offered 'good night' or a variant of it, an obviously well-formed response. Not all of them interpreted it so simply. One offered reminiscence:

My mum had me for a baby, and she says 'go to sleep', and she smacks me when I don't.

and another:

Will you go and tell my Mum something?

Answers like these, highly interesting in terms of the individual child's perceptions of real and imagined circumstances, without being well formed, were rare. In general my expectation that the children would accomplish this first stage quite easily since it related to learning done before schooling starts was met, and I see no reason to doubt the obvious inference — that children at this stage have already learned a great deal not only about the sounds, the vocabulary, and the grammar of their native language, but also a good deal about the discourse of everyday interaction.

The 'Exchanges', designed to uncover individual ability to predict from one *move* to the next in a teaching exchange presented much more difficulty to that youngest group that had, as yet, little experience of the reality — more difficulty, in the event, than the final set of questions that were designed to tap understanding of the situational rules that operate in the classroom. Figure 4 shows the rate of well-formed responses to the cues offered under the heading of 'Exchanges'. The score typically represents text produced by children who told me that a teacher, shown facing her class, holding up a card with a word boldly printed on it was probably initiating an exchange realised by an eliciting move:

What's on this card?

or

Hello. D'you know what this word is? Can you read it?

or

What does this word say?

or

Do you know what this word is?

or, equally plausibly, realised by a directing move, to which Lisa associated an explanation. She was already aware that pupils are expected to pay attention and to be *seen* to do so.

Look at this card. (Because the boy's turning round. He shouldn't.)

It is difficult to suppose that children rising 5, who offer responses like these to a fictitious situation, do not know quite well what is expected in reality. However, their attention to the task was, like their attention to their teacher, intermittent. They typically took only *some* of the opportunities offered by the story to demonstrate the ability to comprehend and participate demonstrated by these answers.

Not all the responses were easy to interpret. It happened quite frequently that in answer to the one above, with the gloss upon it 'and if you were as close to the teacher as the children are, you would see that the card says "dog",' the response was simply, 'dog'. This happened on both sets of visits. Initially it seemed to me that it was not as evidently well-formed discourse as the answers quoted above, and I surmised that those children were unsure what was expected, knew that I looked for an answer, and selected from my question the last item intonationally marked as new information. I still think this is a possible explanation and that it would be useful to look for evidence of its use in naturally occurring classroom situations. There is an alternative explanation though. The answer may simply be elliptical, as classroom talk very often is. It is not at all unusual for teachers to make just such an announcement, and to intend to initiate the exchange by a move that may be directive – 'Notice this word "dog" ', or informing, – 'This says "dog" '. This is one of the ways in which children are taught to associate the spoken with the written word, and to recognise that they are, in an important sense, the same.

Not all the responses that were made could be regarded as well formed. Of the 42 children in the younger group a minority (nine in all) fastened on a single answer, which they repeated in response to every one, irrespective of whether or not it was appropriate. For Kirk and

Neil the stock response was 'hello'. For Sharon it was 'thank you', as though responses learned as routines, which to a child must often seem to function so as to satisfy importunate adults, would serve them here. Lee's stock answer was 'get cross'. Mark's was 'play with it', Michelle's was 'said yes'. On the second visit, the incidence of answers of this sort had noticeably diminished, and it did not occur at all among the 7-year-olds. The stock answers were unexpected and are of some interest. There is an unpublished study by Norman Freeman and his associates (1979) of the non-verbal learning accomplished by much younger children, in their first year of life, that may have a bearing upon it. These children were set a series of tasks involving nesting and stacking cubes. These experimenters found that they would slip into the production of stock responses, apparently unaware of whether or not they were suitable, and that this sort of production was associated with a high degree of rapport between the subject and the observer. Like most teachers, I had been at pains to establish warm and secure relations with these newcomers to schooling. If it is the case that some children, including some who are three years older than those of whom Freeman's observation was made, perceiving between themselves and an initially unfamiliar adult a relationship that is easy and in no way threatening, interpret the situation as one that is not challenging either, one in which immediate and easy, because thoroughly learned, responses will do, then they must, soon after entry to school, discover that they are mistaken. Teachers will, for good educational reasons, not accept such answers. Stock answers are comfortable because they involve the speaker in no sense of risk. They do not commit him. And without commitment or risk of being wrong, there is little chance of significant learning.

It is of course possible that the stock responses some children produced were in another sense the effect of their interpretation of the procedure I adopted. The game I initiated had evidently rules that I, as the adult person responsible for introducing it, already knew. *They* had to learn as they went along. I had my own reasons, not apparent to my subjects, for varying my procedure between children as little as possible. It may be that some of them needed unmistakable feedback from me, and could have made good use of an unmistakable indication that stock responses were *not* acceptable, together with examples of the sort of response I was looking for — a more teacher-like approach, in fact, than at this stage I was ready to adopt.

A smaller subgroup (three in number) responded differently, but in a way which again I did not anticipate. Each began unremarkably, but once well into the task, seemed to reject the deliberately familiar setting and the commonplace narrative in favour of something of their own imagining. In answer to a question similar to that quoted above, Carl said:

She [the teacher] said 'war' and 'sailing' and that's a big red. . . .

From that point, his responses had to do with individuals and their names. A partial coherence characterised Carl's story, but it was a coherence altogether different from mine.

Let's have him a new name — Thomas.
You ain't named Thomas . . . your name. . . .
It ain't Pat — it's Thomas again.

After that, his responses were expected and appropriate as if he had in imagination departed from and subsequently returned to, the matter of shared concern.

Heather's responses, like Carl's, seemed wayward rather than incompetent, as if intermittently she engaged in a verbalisation of her individual and private imagining from which she returned to the classroom when she was ready, and not before providing these responses:

He's dead — and somebody buries him underground.
Is that a real tortoise, and does it walk?

and, at a little later stage, these:

I think you will kick the ball, and play Piggy in the Middle he does
— and get run over — and he has to go to hospital.

The theme of death, and the topic of tortoises, were not done with yet:

Children, why go out and see the tortoise? — and the dog eats the rabbit.

In the night — you die in the night — and you live here. Tell your mum if she comes to get you.

Replies like these, which had no counterpart among those given by the 7-year-old control group, raise a number of interesting questions. It has been cogently argued, and notably by Hasan (1971), that the creative, innovative character of children's language does not consist only, or even most significantly, in their saying what is novel, but in saying what is, in the circumstances, appropriate. These responses were, by the standards which it is natural for an adult to apply, no more than inter- mittently appropriate and partially comprehensible. These three were all talkative children. They enjoyed the task I offered and they were securely in control of the language they required. They had no doubt at all about the alternating nature of conversational interaction, and they took their turn at talking more readily than many children and were more reluctant to relinquish it. They seemed however not to recognise that there was a topic agreed between us that either could change, but only by giving a signal of that intention to the other. There is an obvious difficulty for young children in comprehending that adult understanding, which seems indefinitely to exceed their own, is actually quite limited, and does not include matters so obvious to them as their own changes of mind. They seemed to sense that my invitation to participate in a story-telling activity left them free either to follow the offered lead, or to initiate a narrative or narratives of their own. How children develop a control and a recognition of appropriateness in narrative is clearly a separate study of great interest, and entirely relevant to our understanding of how they interpret what adults say to them. I awaited with particular interest the responses these children would produce after some months' experience of the classroom.

The responses of the newcomers to school bore out the observation often made by teachers that when children represent to themselves and others the circumstances of the classroom, teachers figure as altogether more severe and authoritarian than they are in reality. Where these young children predicted, quite reasonably, negative feedback moves from the teacher, they often expressed disapproval in terms of 'being cross', 'smacking', or 'hitting'. It is unlikely that this was based either on their experience of the first few days of schooling, or of their parents' experience in the 1950s. Teachers of young children have, for much longer than that, seen themselves, and been seen by society, as characterised by patience and gentleness, typically resorting to mild forms of physical constraint only under great provocation as Chatinder's teacher had done. It would be easy to overstate the contrast between the child and the adult view of the matter, but the contrast is there, and seems to indicate an awareness, on the part of newcomers to the educational system, that the world belongs to adults. Power and authority reside in them, and it is important to secure their approval. Children may rarely or never witness the undisguised exercise of power in the classroom, but it is natural to them to represent it in the simplest terms.

The final set of cues I offered was designed to discover to what extent children were aware that meanings have to be interpreted by rules that apply particularly, even if not exclusively, to classroom situations. Both the younger group and the 7-year-olds found less difficulty with this section than with the preceding one in general terms. This was not true of every question. By asking children to demonstrate recognition that a teacher who says to a pupil 'can you . . . do' something, she may intend either a *directive*, requiring the hearer to *react*, or an *elicitation*, requiring a reply, and that the determining factor is the immediate feasibility of complying, I was asking for a subtle appreciation of communicative style. It is not a matter for surprise that all the younger children understood 'can you' as an *eliciting move*, and very few of them were able even on the second occasion to demonstrate understanding that grammatical interrogatives may have a directive function. More than half of them were able to identify the intention of a child shown with hand raised, and of the total sample, ten could offer some explanation of *how* they knew he was bidding for attention.

On all the measures I applied the members of the 7-year-old group did, as one would expect, considerably better, and in identifying the *directive* function of teachers' utterances where function and form were at variance they did very much better. These were, obviously, changes in the anticipated direction. Despite the caution necessary where, whether as teacher or observer, one cannot avoid being 'involved in both deciding what is happening and in making it happen' (Jacobs, 1977), it seemed to me that the story completion activity allowed children to demonstrate perceptions of classroom activity and comprehension of classroom interaction, which may be realised so unevenly and occasionally as to escape the attention even of the careful and alert observer. I felt able at this stage to reach some tentative conclusions. Some of these were negative. I had no evidence of successive discrete stages through which a child moves before emerging as a fully participating pupil. I did find what observation had led me to expect, very wide differences between children not far apart in age. Some could, from the start, accurately predict what would occur from moment to moment in the fictitious classroom, and could show evidence of understanding what teachers mean and what is expected of pupils. Others could do none of these things with any certainty. The effect of these differences must be to produce what I had already observed – a near approximation to a well-formed text of multiple authorship to which only *some* members of the class contribute. I had no evidence bearing on the origin of these differences. Opportunities to learn those situational rules that apply in the classroom, but are not specific to it, must differ between families. Some parents are obviously more teacherly than others in their interaction with their young children. Once schooling starts, the opportunity is available for everyone to learn from rule-governed interaction that is established from the beginning. The child who is uncertain what is meant, or what to say, can exercise the option of silence till he feels confident enough to try. Some eliciting moves will be addressed to him, and there will be many clues to the expected answer and immediate indication of success. He can imitate an answer already given and positively evaluated. (It is noticeable that children often adopt this strategy and are often disappointed at the result). It is a highly favourable learning situation, in part it is the early participation of some of the newcomers that makes it so. The doubt remains of course how far learning to be a participating pupil entails learning to be an independent, well-motivated, learner.

The second series of school visits

These were undertaken in April when the newcomers of the previous September were about to begin their third term of formal schooling. I approached the task with some curiosity, focused upon these questions: would there be evident and substantial differences between the children's responses on the first and on the second occasion? Would the differences among them remain constant? What would I discover, if indeed anything, about those children whose strategies on the first occasion had seemed to deserve especially close scrutiny? Once the series of visits was completed, the children's contributions were inserted into a second grid, so as to make possible comparisons between and among them, and between the second set and the first.

It was to be expected that on the second occasion children would be less shy, readier to respond to an unfamiliar teacher, and better able to follow instructions. It was far from evident what the degree of difference in response to the task would be, whether it would be even or sporadic, or what would be the response of those who had seemed to make very little headway on the first occasion. The most superficial scanning made it clear that the number of unattempted replies was much lower. None of them had, the second time around, a very large number (35 out of a possible 45) of nil responses. Of the children who

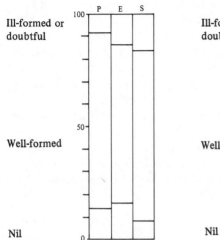

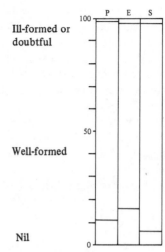

Figure 5
The relative difficulty of
different parts of the task for
the 5-year-olds

Figure 6
The relative difficulty of
different parts of the task for
the 7-year-olds

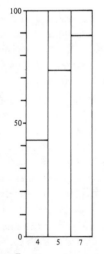

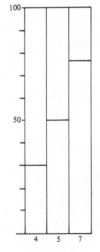

Figure 7
Prediction of appropriate
initiating moves by teachers

Figure 8
Prediction of appropriate
responses by pupils

Based on the mean well formed response to those contexts that require this
prediction, expressed in percentage terms

had seemed very much at a loss on the first occasion two resorted, this time, to stock answers. Two more offered only extremely brief replies – the more noticeable on this second occasion by contrast with most of the other children who were able to give lengthy answers, including varied detail about classroom life. The contrast was (naturally enough) least in the area of Preliminaries, where the cues had elicited a high rate of response on the first occasion. In the set of Exchanges there is a considerable difference between the first and the second set, always in the expected direction, fewer nil responses, fewer that were doubtful, more unmistakably analysable and well formed. The children's ability to recognise the rule-governed, predictable, character of spoken inter-action in the classroom appeared to have increased substantially, nearly to the level of appropriate response I had noticed in my small sample of 7-year-olds (Figures 5 and 6).

Different parts of the exchange did not seem to present different degrees of difficulty (Figures 7 and 8). It was not the case that children found it easier to predict what *children* would say or do, than to pre-dict what *teachers* would say or do. These results indicate that a child who could manage to predict one part of the total exchange plausibly could manage the rest, that is, that the *exchange* rather than the *move* was the natural unit of learning.

In the third group of questions the rate of nil responses was lower again. Few children could discriminate between 'can you?' as an *elicit-ing* and as a *directing* move – though many had at this stage learned to recognise in it a directive function. *Bidding* was understood by virtually everyone, even though it is observable that teachers differ a good deal in when they insist on its regular classroom use. Much of this work simply confirms what observation suggests, and indeed what is apparent to anyone who gives time and thought to the processes of early educa-tion. It does however suggest some possibilities that are not obvious at all. The 5-year-old group did only a little less well than the 7-year-olds. The natural explanation of this is that learning to perform in the pupil role, finding out what to expect, and what is expected, is an important part of the total learning accomplished in the initial months of school-ing, and, further, that it starts at a rapid rate, and continues into the junior school, at a slower pace. The evidence of what claims to be no more than a feasibility study is too slight, and the numbers involved too small, to do more than point to this as something worth additional investigation. It was not evident at the start either how disparate the answers of the youngest children would be, or that on the second occasion even those who had seemed least well able to comprehend would give evidence of some learning accomplished. Relative to the others though, they were still as far, or even further, behind.

Answers were longer, more detailed, and more circumstantial on the second occasion than on the first. There were noticeably fewer references to smacking or hitting. Evidently experience had taught the children how gently, in fact, teachers of that age group usually handle mistakes and misdemeanours. Those responses given on the first occasion by Carl and Mark, and most notably by Heather, in which imagination seemed to slip the leash of the classroom setting, had disappeared virtually without trace. Heather predicted plausible, rule-governed moves, and, as she warmed to the task, she elaborated them more than most children did. Here, for instance, she predicts a teacher's positive feedback move:

> She made him sit on a chair — and he was a good boy, — and she
> gave him some sweets, 'cos he was very good, reading that.

She made Peter, in the story, directed by his teacher to draw a dog, do more than simply *react* by complying; he says:

> I'd like to draw a dog — 'cos I like dogs.

In her story, Tony is unwilling to go and play with the water tray as his teacher directs:

> He says, 'I don't want to, 'cos I don't like getting wet.'

There was no sign of her earlier preoccupation with death and tortoises. The classroom situation was fully comprehensible to her, and capable of engaging her attention for quite long periods, and in her inclusion in her story of reasons for what is said and done, she came close to an explicit recognition of the orderliness of what goes on in classrooms.

A third, teaching visit

The four children initially identified as making almost no response at all were, on the occasion of the second visit, still very much behind the others. Within the ensuing term I planned a third visit to their various schools, in which I would adopt a different, and deliberately didactic stance. I would do my best to teach these children what it is that teachers do, and what it is that they expect. I was encouraged in this by concern about three of the children (Robert, the youngest in my sample being, in this respect, the exception). I had not sought teachers' estimates of individual performance, but it was natural that they should talk to me about the children, about their first impressions, and of the extent to which these were borne out, or not, by later events. It was suggested that Louise would have little to offer me, and explanation was offered in terms of her position in the family — she was the youngest — and she shared their low expectations of her likely attainment. Mark was one of twins, I was told. Both boys were finding the initial adjustment to school difficult. Both had quite severe visual impairment which went a long way to explain their clumsiness in movement. The fleeting and fragmentary nature of Nigel's attention made him a constant focus of disturbance in his classroom. He continually disturbed and upset other children. His teacher coped with him and with the disturbance he caused with an affectionate patience I admired very much.

With this sub-set I planned to use as a teaching aid the Fisher Price Playschool I had put to a different use at an earlier stage. These children were, it seemed to me, unlikely to respond to anything more direct. I hoped I could show them the possibility of identifying with the figures, making them move, and providing them with things to say. Initially, I planned to take the teacher role, and to show that it has more attractive possibilities than any other. Not only has the teacher the best desk and the best chair, she controls the bell and the clock with moveable hands, and she has first claim on the blackboard and the magnetised letters. I hoped I would soon be under some pressure from each of the children to relinquish these privileges in their favour, and that they would gain the beginnings of an understanding of what it is to *elicit* in the expectation of an *answering move*, or to *direct* in expectation of an answering *react*.

The responses I got were neither expected nor uniform. Neither Nigel, nor Robert, nor Mark, was willing to play with the materials in the way I had anticipated. The items that could be noisily manipulated caught their attention. When I invited attention to the desks and chairs and suggested a game of school, they disregarded my suggestions as having no meaning for them. They quickly wearied of a toy which had initially attracted them, and looked for something else. It seemed that for them the figures of the teacher and the pupils and the school furnishings and equipment had no representative or symbolic function.

Louise responded quite differently. When I arrived for my third visit, her teacher told me to expect a changed, and much happier, little girl. In the interval since my second visit, Louise had learned to read with a rapidity and success that gave the lie to everyone's expectation that she was the slow one. Reward followed — not just pleasure and approval, but a hymn book of her own — a privilege that awaited any child on attaining a reading age of 7, and that, used daily in assembly, signalled that achievement to the world. In one respect Louise defeated my expectation too. I had expected the Playschool would have the attraction of novelty. Louise claimed (and I believe her) to have been given such a toy for Christmas. Her play with it may therefore have been rehearsed rather than spontaneous. She, like the other three, was quite unwilling to accept me as a playmate and turned a deaf ear to my offer of a shared make-believe game. Without delay, she unpacked the box, set the pupils in rows of desks with the teacher facing them, and assumed the teacher role.

You've got to write your names out proper!

she announced authoritatively. Moments later, turning to me, she said,

The teacher's got to go to a meeting.

And, as she removed the teacher to the top of a box, out of sight of the class,

This little girl is going to be the teacher.

However, the delegation of authority was not a success:

They've been very naughty,

she told me, with a good deal of relish, adding,

All of them have been very naughty. These children are doing very naughty,

and then, lowering her voice confidentially,

The teacher's talking to thin air!

Her school day was punctuated by the ringing of the bell for 'playtime' and 'home time', and at the end she carefully and quickly packed up the toys and asked my permission to return to her classroom. Louise sustained her make-believe in telling herself a story, and she used the toy pieces to support and illustrate her narrative. She gave clear evidence that she understood the teacher's roles to a much greater degree than I had anticipated. She recognised that the teacher does not only organise and control — she has duties that may remove her from the classroom altogether. 'Being a teacher' was for Louise, within about eight months of starting full-time schooling, a role capable of being assumed temporarily by someone whose usual part was that of pupil, and its obligations might be successfully or unsuccessfully discharged. 'Good' children react to a teacher's *directives* as she expects: naughty children disregard clearly understood *directives*. Good teachers get compliance; unlucky pupils, assigned the role of the teacher, do not. Neither the teacher nor her deputy was represented by Louise as *informing* pupils or *eliciting* answers, but clearly one must be cautious of inferring that these functions of a teacher were therefore not perceived. In order to *represent* them it is necessary to identify some areas of the speaker's knowledge and experience as potentially, but not actually, shared by others; 5-year olds give no evidence of being able to do this at all readily, nor would one expect that they should.

The experimental teaching situation I had set up was in some respects disappointingly unproductive. Louise had already learned all I hoped to teach. Robert and Mark and Nigel were unresponsive to what I offered. Like their respective teachers, I encountered the intractable difficulty of securing their unstable attention, and the toys I offered seemed not to have for them the meaning I assumed. While it is not of course true that because I failed in my efforts to assist children who seemed especially slow to learn they could not be taught, the experience gave no support to the supposition that it might be possible to identify those children for whom learning to be participant pupils was particularly difficult, and to intervene by teaching them, in a deliberate way, what others learn without such assistance. Where there is a compulsory age of entry to full-time schooling classrooms are bound to include some children who simply have not reached a stage of development at which they can learn what is appropriate for the majority. This is in itself not so much a matter for concern as the possibility that opportunities to learn may not recur, and that the experience of failure to learn may do subtle and cumulative damage. Whether children generally would benefit if teachers were made aware of the predictable and rule-governed character of the interaction that goes on in classrooms is another question altogether. If they had that awareness, developed in pre- or in in-service training, they would find it natural to make their intentions and expectations more explicit than they often do. Teachers already expect to insist upon whatever routine for registration they prefer, and to teach a class to bid for the right to answer. They expect that their teaching will require repetition at intervals over a period of time. The possibility of interpreting much more broadly the need to give attention to teaching what will assist children to find their classroom environment comprehensible and predictable seems well worth pursuing.

I had at this stage to review what I had learned about classroom language by designing and trying out, with a small sample, but one in principle capable of being extended, a cloze procedure for discourse. What I observed earlier was confirmed: newcomers do not start at a common level of ignorance and inexperience. While much learning how to interact is done in the initial months of schooling, it is also true that learning is done at different rates and occurs in sudden spurts, so that extremely different degrees of understanding persist among children who entered school at the same time. School organisation, curricula, and textbooks are organised on the supposition that understanding increases steadily, by a process of accretion, so that the realities of learning – that the rate differs between children who had no starting-point in common, that some children may seem to make no headway at all, and then lurch towards understanding – are seen as deviant rather than characteristic of the learning process. The requirements made by the materials I used need further to be checked against individual classroom performance, and against other evidence, such as individual progress in literacy. Both sorts of check are important, since those children who perform well on a story-telling task are likely to include some who are, at an early stage, ready participants, and some who understand perfectly well what is going on and what is expected, but are, temperamentally or for a variety of other reasons, reluctant to speak. It is *this* group of children that I hope might be the eventual beneficiaries of the developed work. Their number is not small, and while it is to be expected that their difficulties will diminish over time there can be no certainty that this will be so. They are the children about whom teachers regularly express concern that, taking little overt part in class, seeking, as they seem to do, to avoid notice, they may be and remain unaware of what they *could* do. Some children are naturally rather taciturn. Teachers are right to recognise that in classrooms such pupils are vulnerable, not just because their teachers naturally enough look for responsiveness and dislike its contrary, but because it is extremely difficult for teachers to know what to expect of unresponsive pupils. A straightforward procedure, that could be carried out by any teacher in a position to devote twenty minutes to an individual pupil, and that would discriminate between a silent child for whom the classroom was a confusion of unpredictable events, and one for whom it was, in essentials, orderly and comprehensible, would, I believe, be worth having, and would justify the expenditure of some resources.

8

Retrospect:
implications of the study for
teachers and future teachers

A final chapter has necessarily a partially retrospective character: I shall begin this one by outlining the extent to which I hope in the remaining pages to look back, and to look forward. The chapter falls into two parts. In the first I want to focus upon what has, in the preceding chapters, been stated or implied, that discourse is systematic and its structure is predictive, and that these related concepts, that might at a superficial view be dismissed as altogether too abstract and general in character to be interesting to anybody except committed professional linguists, are, on the contrary, productive of insights that teachers can put directly to use. In discourse expectations are set up, are tested, and are confirmed (or not) and then, with the next unit, the next exchange, the cycle starts again. Much of what has gone before has to do with this process, and with what can be observed of the way newcomers to a particular sort of situated discourse learn to participate in it, to know what to expect and what is expected. There is some evidence that the expectations that are transmitted are remarkably durable. The predictive structure of discourse is recognisable in the text produced by teachers and learners of different ages, in varying situations, and despite all the differences of topic and presentation, the acquisition of specialised vocabulary, and the use of very much more complicated grammatical construction, that attend the passage from the reception classroom to the sixth form and beyond. Further, there is some evidence, and I shall want to examine it, that the structure of classroom discourse resists change between the generations, and shares the conservatism that has often been noticed as characteristic of educational processes generally. Some evidence may be available in answer to the question: how are expectations transmitted? how does it come about that they are so durable in the face of serious and well-publicised and deliberate efforts to modify them?

In the second part of the chapter I shall attempt retrospect and summary. I set myself to pursue the question posed by the authors of TAD:

How does the five year old who speaks when he wants to become the ten year old who waits to be nominated? (p. 113)

Such partial and incomplete answers as I believe I have to offer need to be set out, even though they require to be heavily qualified. Indeed, I do not think the question quoted above can be answered exactly as it is posed, but neither do I think it altogether defies serious enquiry, and the further questions that investigation poses deserve to be pursued. In addition methods of enquiry are of interest to other researchers. I found observation, including participant observation, indispensable, but not sufficient. Observation has limitations, some inherent, some practical but extremely difficult to overcome in practice, even if not in principle. Alternative approaches, and deliberate efforts to elicit the sort of data that are required in order to take the investigation to the next stage have their limits too; they supplement rather than supersede observation. False starts in research are often less unproductive than they seem at the time; even when they are disappointing, they have some interest for teacher-researchers, working within the constraints that classrooms impose. I hope to highlight those parts of the study that seem to me directly relevant to the work of teachers and others who make decisions about what happens in classrooms. Finally, having been for a long time involved with the pre-service and in-service studies undertaken by teachers, I should be sorry if I felt I had nothing to say to people concerned with this difficult and important indirect service to children in schools.

To claim, as I have done, that learning to participate as a comprehending pupil is essentially a matter of learning to predict, to anticipate within rather narrow limits, what normally and typically is going to happen from moment to moment, is, in effect, simply to assert the claim that distinguishes the Birmingham model from others currently in use. It is different in being linguistically motivated. It does not make claim to finality or completeness. It has already been subjected to a number of important revisions, and may well be further modified. What is unchanged from the stage at which those responsible for the model made it publicly available for use is the assertion that the underlying organisation of discourse, of which classroom discourse is an interesting variant, is a linguistic organisation, that is to say a predictive organisation. Participants take turns in setting up expectations; understanding means interpreting clues and making guesses, and the knowledge that users of the language share of the regularities in it ensures that the process is principled and rapid. Prediction may be more or less certain of course; language use can surprise users, and this is at least as often the source of enjoyment as it is of dismay. Classroom discourse typically sets up well-defined expectations, including the expectation on the part of the participant who responds to a teacher's eliciting move that the response will get immediate feedback. He will *know* if his response was in accord with the teacher's expectation. In this last respect, the structure of classroom discourse typically differs from that of discourse between participants having more equal rights and obligations. Where feedback is part of the structure there is no need for subtle processes of inference to know if the last utterance was satisfactory to the other speaker, and it is natural to suppose that such directness is helpful to the school pupil who is, by comparison with his teacher, a relatively inexperienced member of the speech community. The recognition that the structure of language is organised at every level so as to make partial prediction possible, to recognise that to be a user of a language is to operate the rules so as to set up expectations and to predict in your turn – this seems to me necessary information for teachers to have. As practised, sophisticated and literate language users, there is of course an important sense in which they are already in possession of it, independently of anything they may have learned in the course of their professional preparation. Knowledge that is deliberately acquired, fully conscious, capable of being verbalised, knowledge of the sort that has traditionally been acquired by the professional person, is however different from that which is assimilated in the process of becoming a member of a culture. It is, for one thing, more flexible in use. Its application to new and unfamiliar situations can be monitored. It can be subjected to processes of criticism as fresh experience, or new evidence, becomes available. Recognition of the linguistic structure of discourse is not particularly easily or quickly acquired, but it seems to me not at all difficult to demonstrate that it is professionally useful to the teacher – useful enough, I would claim, to justify the time it requires. It is an area of knowledge and understanding that relates directly to the daily, commonplace, entirely unavoidable elements of the teacher's work, and it makes possible an understanding of those elements that allows deliberate and positive (as opposed to unthinking and habitual) use of them. By emphasising what children in classrooms are required to do with language, and the demands made of their understanding of linguistic structures, it serves as a reminder of what are the inescapable prerequisites of learning. Unless they share a language code with their teacher, most of the clues that she provides are simply unavailable to them. Some strategy has then to be found – an interpreter used, a language learned by the teacher, non-verbal communication extensively and consistently used, and delay (relative to a situation where a shared language is available) has to be anticipated and allowed for. Even in what appear to be favourable circumstances it is useful to be reminded of the need to provide *enough* opportunities to make predictions. There are principled reasons for extending the redundancy present in language by the deliberate inclusion of repetition, paraphrase, and reminders, and for supplementing verbal with other sorts of communication. In addition, language use in classrooms is more than simply a concern of teachers. Public interest is keen. Teachers are obliged to come to terms with advice, criticism and suggestions from many sources. Whether these often incompatible counsels are experienced as stimulating and thought-provoking, or as contradictory and harassing, depends in great part on whether teachers are in a position to evaluate advice on a principled basis, and to articulate, and justify, their response. There is for example currently an emphasis on the prime need for participation and involvement in learning. This is welcome in itself; it is however harassing to the teacher who feels uneasy at assembling children and talking while they (for the most part) listen, or briefly respond. Most teachers, including teachers of quite young children, find they cannot easily avoid doing this, not, certainly, for long periods, and do so frequently and regularly. They need to know, and to be able to defend, the contention that the appearance of simple passivity on the children's part is illusory; that these sessions are circumstances in which there is opportunity for children to predict what is going to happen, to classify as they go along, to notice, and to repair mistakes. They are, I believe, assisted in a number of entirely ordinary, but necessary and responsible kinds of classroom work by recognition of it in these terms.

Knowing about discourse, and knowing, in more general terms, about the organisation of language, is not, and should not be presented as, a panacea. In order to make a claim effectively it is necessary to state clearly what are its limits. It is easy to think of a wide range of educational problems deserving of urgent attention – claims related to the allocation of resources, for example, or of pupils' motivation to learn, to which the analysis of classroom discourse makes no contribution. The contention that good work is done, and has always been done, by teachers whose repertoire of skills and knowledge includes no conscious and articulate knowledge about the organisation of language, is beyond dispute. There is a more persuasive assumption that does need to be examined – the assumption, usually unspoken, that knowledge is relevant and useful in so far as it makes troublesome and difficult tasks easier. Something like the contrary seems to me nearer the mark. Principled understanding, in the area of language use as in any other, tends to make problematic what was formerly taken for granted, and, to that extent at least, to increase its perceived difficulty. With these reservations I would none the less claim that an understanding of the linguistic organisation of the interaction between teacher and taught makes available to the teacher an explicit recognition of what she does and what they do, indicates a need for alternative strategies and the limits within which these are practicable, and makes possible a critical evaluation of her own work and of the external trends, influences, and pressures that bear upon it.

The durable character of classroom language

There is some evidence that the structure of classroom discourse is highly resistant to change. I found a close approximation, in classrooms for the youngest children, to the structure (though not, obviously, to the topics of the vocabulary) characteristic of those upper-primary classrooms which provided the original data base for the Birmingham model. The text produced in secondary classrooms is readily analysable in similar terms, and suggests this interesting question: to what extent, and for how long, is it *possible* for teachers to change the structure at will? Efforts to do so are, of course, regularly made. They can be observed in classrooms for young children where many teachers, seeking to give their pupils the opportunity of extended (as distinct from habitually brief and hesitant) responding moves, institute 'News Time'. In such sessions teachers do not relinquish their controlling role. The initiating and feedback moves are theirs, but they typically address a series of reinitiating moves, including *prompts* and *clues* to the same individual, so as to secure as long and detailed a contribution as possible. *Feedback moves* are held in reserve, and when they are offered, the warmth of approval is related to the length of the response. The structure of the discourse is modified rather than radically changed. Teachers of older students seek, for readily understood educational reasons, to set up a situation where students take initiatives and look to the group, rather than to any one individual, for feedback. Classes often bear the name of seminar, and, rather less often, the verbal interaction that goes on is observably different in its organisation from that of the classroom. However, this is rarely easy to achieve, and sometimes defeats serious and sustained efforts on the part of the person responsible for the organisation of the class. No doubt the reason is in part that the habits of associating the educational process with a particular discourse structure are very deeply internalised and, in the absence of explicit recognition, are not amenable to change. Students in the early stages of tertiary education often have real difficulty in envisaging that learning could occur within a discourse structure different from that to which they are accustomed. They are unwilling to take initiatives in these circumstances, although in other sorts of situated discourse, they do so without hesitation and would interpret reluctance as evidence of some personal attribute, like extreme shyness. They assume further, that the option which the organisation of classroom discourse makes available to all participants *except* the teacher, the option of silence, is available to them. By exercising that option, they impose a very strong pressure upon the lecturer to assume the teacher role. One part of that role he actually shares, not only with the teacher in the classroom or the chairman in the committee, and that is the obligation to break a silence that has persisted long enough to be socially embarrassing. He is, inescapably, the *residual speaker*. He finds himself, however unwillingly, eliciting the response he hoped would be offered spontaneously, making informing moves that he hoped would come from those present, and often meeting the evident expectation that he should provide feedback to answering moves, engaged in a discourse structurally indistinguishable from that of the classroom. Habit is not enough to explain why the wish to change should not be sufficient to effect it. The different rights and responsibilities of speakers relate to their perceived position in a social hierarchy. Where students perceive themselves as newcomers, relative to the lecturer who is on his home ground, uninformed in areas where he is experienced, uncertain of their status in an institution where he is a salaried employee, and is perhaps highly regarded, they perceive him as having the rights and responsibilities that go with the superordinate position. Where the asymmetry is not so evident – the lecturer is for example a young newcomer, and plainly unsure of his ground, or the students are assured and mature people, the difficulty of initiating and sustaining a discourse *not* that of the classroom is much less.

There is another, less obvious sense, in which the structure of classroom discourse seems to resist change. The experience of schooling has been part of our shared culture for a long time. Representations of that experience in fiction and in the metaphors commonly employed in talk about it, suggest that it is represented and remembered as organised, not random, and as involving participants who are unalike, having dissimilar roles and rights and interests. This is the representation that teachers bring to the classroom independently of what they may have learned in the course of professional training. The children in my sample, who found it natural to verbalise teachers' disapproval or disappointment in terms of 'smacking' or 'hitting', brought to their first experience of schooling expectations they had already formed and which, unless my evidence is unrepresentative, they quite soon modified as they gained experience of the reality. In their chapter on 'The child and authority', Opie and Opie (1967) cite a number of songs and rhymes that have currency among the child population independently of printed sources. These present teachers as the natural opponents of children, ineffectual and ridiculous figures for the most part, unfairly paid for the work they require pupils to do, taking pleasure in their license to punish rebels against their dubious authority. School stories present an essentially similar picture. They seem (perhaps temporarily) in abeyance, but comics survive, and those most often bought, read, and shared by children at the primary stage of schooling regularly include stories about schools, teachers and pupils, and as regularly represent the relation between them as a guerrilla warfare. The teacher is an ineffectual Goliath, forever harassed by numerous, devious, quick-witted, and ruthless Davids. Readers of the *Beano* are invited to identify with broadly delineated stereotypes, Dennis the Menace, or Roger the Dodger. The Bash Street Kids are a rebel gang, and the action is concerned with the bumbling efforts of their teacher to get them to school and into enemy territory. Their teacher cuts a sorry figure, bewildered, bespectacled, and inseparable from his mortar board — an item of ritual dress that has become a rarity anywhere, and has never been part of the world of primary schools. He does little more than protest at the gang's activities, which are presented as bold, ingenious, and daring. Roger is not a figure to be admired or identified with. He has neither talent nor application for anything except cheating his teacher, who, true to stereotype, is balding, middle-aged and gullible. With all these advantages, Roger is a ludicrously unsuccessful rogue. The broad joke lies in presenting the classroom as the scene of a battle, endlessly renewed, that neither side has the wit to win. An essentially similar image remains vividly present to contemporary adult imagination in the work of Dickens and others. Dotheboys Hall and Salem

House, the fictitious Rugby of *Tom Brown's Schooldays*, and the fifth form at St. Dominic's are part of our shared culture, schools where conflict is endemic, where teachers utilise their advantages, adulthood, strength, authority, licensed violence against boys, who pit against these forces superior numbers and superior wits. All these are stories designed for boys. Publications designed for girls display an interesting variant. There is a general absence of knockabout farce. The tone is altogether quieter, and the stories are, to an overwhelming degree, variations on the theme of the Ugly Duckling. The heroines with whom readers are invited to identify may come from undistinguished homes, their beauty and their talent may be unrecognised – but not for long. They speedily attain recognition, typically in one of a rather small range of agreeably conspicuous activities. Success – as ballerinas, or horsewomen, or actresses – is the outcome; the school is not a battle-field, but an arena for the display of accomplishment, and the heroine has often an ally and admirer in a sympathetic teacher. Her struggle is against uncomprehending, and often hostile, classmates and family, who are obliged in the end to award her due of recognition, even of adulation.

Mock warfare, and competition having an element of make-believe, resemble each other, and are persuasive metaphors for the realities of the classroom in that they allow for the confrontation of opposing interests and of dissimilar roles. Well-understood conventions, articulated as the rules of fair play, govern both. We seem a long way from exhausting the sense that it is natural to represent the processes associated with schooling in these terms. The metaphor I have used on a number of occasions (following *TAD* in this) is that of a game. It is a metaphor not too far removed from that of conflict or competition, and it is a natural metaphor to use of ordered, partially predictable activity, into which adults who are very familiar with the regularities that make it so, initiate newcomers, who have to learn what these are. Like the metaphors of conflict and contest, this one allows for conflicting interests and for elements of competition. These features of society are certainly present in classrooms. They are not however their most prominent or central or significant features – nor are they ideally of games. Participation (as players are regularly reminded) is what matters, not winning and losing. The conventions and regularities, the rules that the players agree to be bound by – these constitute the game. If these are observed, the game can be played in a great variety of circumstances, including circumstances that are very far from ideal. Any small object that comes to hand can substitute for a chess piece. Cricket can be played on a beach with a rubber ball and makeshift stumps. There are quite narrow limits, however, on the makeshift modifications that are possible without changing the nature of the game. We speak naturally of the same game played on innumerable occasions, different in every respect except the crucial one — that the same set of rules that constitute the organisation of the game are observed. Individuals may, and do, break the rules, and the normal penalty is exclusion. They are taken to have opted out of play. Breaking the rules does not change them; change is possible but is slow, difficult and piecemeal. Games are very durable features of our experience; they resist change. It is a natural metaphor to use, and a variously applicable one, one of the 'metaphors we live by' (in the phrase Lakoff and Johnson use as their title of a study of the role of metaphor in language). It certainly provides an analogy for the observable processes of learning to participate in classroom discourse. Children learn to be classroom pupils as they learn from adults to take part in a variety of suitable and enjoyable games. Adult players almost never tell them, except in quite partial and limited ways, what the rules of a new game are. This is a difficult undertaking, both for the person who tries to frame the rules and for the person who attempts to interpret them, and is regarded as in any case unnecessary. The newcomer to the game is encouraged to take part. Experienced players expect him to make clumsy and ineffectual moves, and they do not take advantage of his ineptitude as they would do of the mistakes and hesitations of a more nearly equal opponent. Instead, they play their own role, reciprocal to his, but at nothing like the limit of their actual skill, taking time and opportunity to suggest and prompt and encourage. Very fine judgment is needed, for the novice in such a situation begins quite soon to perceive what is required, and to get confidence and skill in doing it, and the adult player has to shift between assisting and opposing him. There seems to me to be a clear and rather exact analogy between the behaviour of adults teaching children games and the way in which I observed teachers interact with newcomers to the classroom. Something like this seems to be implied by the way in which Sinclair and Coulthard express the question that prompted the writing of this book: how, they ask, is *bidding* learned? and it is to a summary of what it seems to me I learned in pursuit of that question that I turn now.

Learning to be a pupil: a summary

I have said I do not think the question can be answered as directly as Sinclair and Coulthard pose it, nor without some preliminary qualification. The example they give is that of learning to *bid*, to raise a hand in response to a teacher's eliciting move to signal readiness to make a responding move, and to wait to be nominated before speaking, or alternatively, to allow someone else to respond, and the teacher to provide feedback, without interrupting. *Bidding* seems to be selected as an example of the operation of rules that obtain in classrooms and are not a feature of other sorts of situated discourse. In one respect though it is not typical. Teachers are aware that bidding has this in common with routines of registration and distribution – children will probably not have encountered any of these before entering school. Teachers expect to choose a suitable time to introduce each of these, to instruct children in whatever variant they prefer, and to repeat the lesson, or reminders of it, at rather frequent intervals. Teachers are not in general terms aware of the predictable and rule-governed character of exchanges, and I have already argued that there would be significant professional advantages for them in becoming so. Children are not explicitly taught, for example, that lessons include subdivisions, and that the fresh start is regularly and recognisably signalled. Nor do teachers indicate to children that at the start of a lesson they can expect to hear, and should listen for a headline, an announcement about what will follow, which will help them to understand quickly and clearly. It is easy to suppose that these features of discourse structure could be made as easily familiar to children as is *bidding*, and with as little use of technical terms, but, for well-understood reasons, they are not. Learning to bid is made easy; learning to recognise and classify teachers' initiatives as the lesson goes along, learning that teachers rarely evaluate a response in an unmistakably negative way, and that uncertain or non-committal evaluation is to be interpreted as negative, learning that a question asked by a teacher about a forbidden activity is to be understood as an instruction to stop doing it – all these have normally to be learned *without* the assistance that straightforward statement, suitably expressed and repeated where necessary, might provide.

Further, children do not share a starting-point of total inexperience. Playgroups and nursery classes familiarise some, but not all, new-comers to formal schooling with what it is to be one of many children, of approximately the same age, assembled in one place, with equal rights to all sorts of shared resources, including the attention of adults.

If, as seems certain, the ability to *attend* is a prerequisite of learning, it is inevitable that at any given chronological age it will be better developed in some children than in others. I encountered in my sample a minority who seemed as yet unable to attend for long enough to learn. English children have to learn new uses of the mother tongue they have learned in a domestic setting; those who have learned a mother tongue not that of their teacher must start by learning a new language from exposure to a set of uses of that language that are unfamiliar. Despite the formidable character of that requirement they do unmistakably bring to the classroom well-founded and helpful expectations. Like English children, they expect adults to make decisions and set limits on what they may do, to take the lead, and to show affection and approval. They attend to the clues to meaning that are present in the context, and which the teachers use fully and emphatically. Some partial understanding of the function of teachers' initiating moves was possible even where knowledge of other language levels – of vocabulary and of grammatical structures for example, was negligible.

Among children for whom there is no such language barrier there are observable differences in the rate at which they learn to predict and to classify teachers' utterances just as there are differences in learning rate generally. The discourse characteristic of teachers is not confined to the classroom. Parents teach children, and adopt a recognisably didactic discourse structure when they do so. It must be the case that some parents do so more often, and perhaps more memorably, than others. The published transcripts of talk in the homes of 3-year-olds, collected by the Bristol-based project on Language at Home and at School, includes a number of examples of overtly didactic discourse between parents and their pre-school children. Parents were made welcome in all the classrooms to which I had access, as part of a serious and determined effort to reassure new pupils and to engage parents' sympathies with educational processes and purposes. On one occasion, when a mother brought along a child to spend the afternoon with the children in the class that he was soon to join, the teacher introduced me to her as 'someone who was very interested in children's language'. This mother, understandably in the circumstances, interpreted the introduction to mean that I would like the little boy to display his linguistic accomplishments. The child was as reluctant to do so as children usually are, and in persuading him, his mother made initiating moves, and provided a *prompt* and a *clue*:

Mother: You recite that nursery rhyme.
Child: What?
Mother: You know. 'Dr Foster went to Gloucester.' Would you say that?

The child provided the expected response, not quite correctly —

Child: Dr Foster went to Gloucester
In a shower of rain —
An' never went there again.

— and got feedback from the unmistakable pride in his mother's voice.

Mother: He says that to all our friends. Don't you? He says that to all of them.

She tried again, but shyness or strangeness or simple failure of recall ensured that the child was silent despite several efforts at reinitiation. This was analysable didactic discourse approximating fairly closely to that which he was soon to experience in the classroom. It must resemble the experience of many children, probably of most children, but in varying degrees, and it differs from teacher talk in one significant respect, that a parent, teaching a child, does not at the same time have responsibility for the safety and good behaviour of a class. Discourse features that relate to the control of many participants by one of their number, probably are unique to the classroom and unfamiliar to newcomers. *Bidding* is one such feature, and so are the extended transactions that occur when teachers elicit responses from a representative and fairly large sample of those present — sometimes from each of them. The question how is learning to participate in classroom discourse accomplished has to start from an acknowledgment that learners have very different experiences at entry; they do not start level and they learn in general rapidly, but at different rates. At any one time a satisfactorily responding class, creating well-formed, analysable text in collaboration with the teacher, is comprised of individuals whose actual degree of comprehending participation is extremely various. Some of the learning that is required is directly and explicitly taught. Most of it is not. There are however very many clues, verbal and non-verbal, to assist the learner. What he must know, in order as it were to gain a foothold, is not formidably extensive. The limited nature of the responding role, the fact that nearly all the initiatives are for the teacher to take, ensures that. Teachers assist, not by explaining what the rules are, but by providing *prompts* and *clues*, by an initial tolerance of very hesitant and partial responses, by supplying suitable responses where inexperienced pupils seem quite at a loss for them. The disparities among pupils of the same standing are themselves helpful to the slowest and least confident. They offer models to imitate, and children do very often offer responses that clearly enough imitate those that have recently been offered and have seemed to please the teacher well enough to get positive feedback. This sort of imitation is not by any means always well received. Teachers are often irritated by it, and a second or third responding move that evidently imitates the first is as a rule evaluated less favourably. Imitation, doing what the others do, may none the less be an important first step towards understanding just enough of what is happening to be able to engage in initial, tentative, participation.

The model of discourse and the methods of enquiry

Some part of this retrospect needs to be given to summarising those parts of the enquiry that may interest researchers, or teachers who include a commitment to research in their understanding of their role. I made use of a linguistically motivated model of situated discourse that made no claim to finality — indeed the period during which I have worked with the 1975 model has been one of rapid and important theoretical development — but did claim to have reached a stage where it could be applied to analytic uses not necessarily envisaged by those responsible for its design. Simply to demonstrate that the coding system derived from it is applicable to text different from that which provided the initial data base for its designers is of course a necessary task which has been done here and elsewhere. If the system were *not* variously applicable one of two conclusions would, so far as I can see, be inevitable; either the claim to describe the discourse organisation of the classroom could not be sustained, or the structure must differ, between classrooms and between texts. However, the experience of coding texts points in the same direction as other evidence, it indicates a structure capable of extremely various realisations and resistant to change. My hope was to go further than demonstrating that the coding system is very variously applicable.

The central, essential feature of the Birmingham model is its assertion, supported by description in some detail, of the orderly, predictable, rule-governed character of discourse. Like other levels of language, its organisation makes it interpretable. The expectations set up are those of meaning in a context of use. The process by which children learn to recognise and take part in this collaborative activity was the one I set out to study, and I started by observation in classrooms that I knew would provide a great quantity of data. The problem I met was the anticipated one – that the quantity rapidly assembled would be extremely large, but its character would be fragmentary. As I began to formulate questions in a more specific way, I became aware of the elusive nature of the evidence that I required. For all that, I believe participant observation, apart from being the most readily available strategy, is a powerful and indeed an indispensable one. It gives access to the variety and abundance of text; it offers constant reminders of the unexpectedness, repetitiveness, untidiness of the data. It obliges the researcher to recognise the inevitability of some distortion as the effect of his own contribution, and it imposes caution in interpretation. It is a kind of natural history, modest, old-fashioned, and entailing a minimum of disturbance to the environment of the subject of study. Its possibilities are not easily exhausted.

My experience of finding that I needed to supplement observation is, I think, a very common one, and my experience of false starts may well be commoner than is often acknowledged. I needed an approach I would control, and one that would be in principle applicable to a randomly selected sample of whatever size the available resources would allow. Some variant of a cloze procedure was a natural choice. Cloze procedure has become an accepted and well-tried way of testing subjects' knowledge at other levels – and that for good reason. It directly depends on the way speakers and hearers use language at every level of its organisation. The learner is confronted with incomplete text. On the basis of his understanding he has to supply what is missing. The measure of his success in what the native speaker would do on the basis of his knowledge and the degree of that success offers a clear and useful indication of the extent to which his knowledge approximates to that of a native. If (and only if) a researcher has access to a linguistically motivated description of language at the level of discourse, there is nothing to hinder the construction and interpretation of a device for completing a cloze test at that level, and using it as a measure of the extent to which learners approximate to the performance of an experienced participant. The incomplete story is a first attempt to construct such a test, and the form it takes is just a device for making a cloze procedure comprehensible by, and acceptable to, very young subjects.

It seemed to me sufficiently practicable and flexible in use to deserve revision and refinement with a view to more extended trial. The researcher has control over what is deleted, and therefore what subjects must supply, and the linguistic description from which the test derives also makes possible a principled interpretation of the effects of its use. The development of cloze procedures at other levels has significantly contributed to the detailed, fair, and accurate measurement of new language learning. All sorts of practical advantages accrue from this to teachers and taught, and at the same time cloze procedures furnish researchers having a special interest in new language learning with a well-developed tool. Comparable interest in the post-initial stages of first language acquisition, including learning about situated language use, is well established – a research activity having a range of important applications. The development of a linguistic description of discourse organisation, in contexts of situated language use, is important (among other reasons) because it creates the conceptual framework within which new tools for investigation can be developed.

My efforts to study children's make-believe play were disappointing and unproductive, as was my attempt to assist, by means of initiating play, those children who seemed slowest to learn. The observation of make-believe is potentially a rich source of information since it must derive directly from their representation of their experience to themselves; it offers a window on their perceptions. The very characteristics that make it so potentially informative – its spontaneity, its privacy, seem to me, in retrospect, to impose conditions on its use that many researchers, and I was of their number, cannot meet. Children are aware of a stranger's presence – indeed there is no attempt at all to conceal the stranger from them, and it is not difficult to establish a relation of tolerance and even liking. Make-believe play needs more than that – it requires a degree of trust that takes time to develop. Its observation and interpretation are simply not available to outsiders. The positive aspect of this disappointment is the confirmation that there is a mode of observation, a tool of research uniquely available for observers who combine with the role of researcher that of teacher or of parent.

Some implications of the study for the education of teachers

If there are reasons why teachers need to know about situated language use, then there is clearly a case for making room for the study of the topic in the course of pre-service training, and for ensuring that sufficient opportunities occur to supplement or to extend that knowledge at a later stage. In general terms this position is widely acceptable and needs no defence. It bears more than one interpretation however. The claim is made that what teachers require, in order to understand the spoken texts in which they participate, to use books, at every level of the educational process, and to respond appropriately to the written texts they require pupils to produce, is a sympathetic and sensitive application of the knowledge that, as literate users of English, they already have – and that this is enough. The study of linguistically motivated models at any level, it is argued, involves coming to terms with difficult abstractions. These are not easy to comprehend or to apply. They are an unattractive topic to many potentially excellent teachers, and are simply not comprehensible to some of them. At best, they require a substantial investment of time and energy that could be put to other and better use. The resources required are, at present and in a foreseeable future of financial constraint, simply not available. This position, which I have tried not to misrepresent, is the contrary of that implied in this book. I would not however contest what is obviously true, that the practical difficulties of furthering any change are great where there is severe financial constraint that has, with other factors, borne heavily on teacher education. However I want, in concluding what I have to say about language in early schooling, to make briefly the case for the inclusion in the training of teachers of a substantial element, designed to familiarise them with a model of language that gives particular attention to those rules that operate above the level of the sentence, not only on the grounds, already argued, that they have in the longer term, a professional need for such information, but on the grounds that in the immediate term it is information that could make the training process more effective.

Teaching practice, carried out in schools, is a component of every course of training; it is the component that is as a rule regarded by everyone involved as central, and it engages a very high level of commitment from nearly all students. It contributes a major element to success in courses leading (subject to satisfactory completion of the probationary year) to qualified teacher status. Much effort is expended by training institutions and by schools, in securing good learning opportunities for future teachers. The quality of that experience is none the less very variable, for many reasons outside the control of those most closely concerned. Supervision is very important, for the learning opportunities it presents, and as a basis of assessment, and responsibility is shared between lecturers who in this function represent the institution, and teachers who delegate to students some of their ordinary teaching duties. Teachers see more of the student and his work: lecturers see relatively little of each single student, but they can claim to have an overview of the levels attained and the difficulties experienced by many students in a variety of schools, and as a rule the responsibility for assessing the student belongs to them. Students are seen teaching, at longer or shorter intervals, by lecturers, and receive, verbally or in writing, a record of their impressions, together with comment, critical or commendatory, and as a rule suggestions for addition or improvement. My observation of this established practice is that observation and comment is rarely less than detailed, thoughtful, and fully cognisant of the additional strains that the process imposes upon the student, and that the interaction between lecturer and student is often perceptive and generous on the one part, receptive and appreciative on the other. Even at best, however, it is a matter of impressionistic comment; it is, and is seen as, selective and even arbitrary. In some courses of training these elements are reduced, by the recording of lessons for subsequent and more detailed comment by the student concerned and by others, who may include the lecturer, or by the use of a coding system, of which FIAC, or a variant of it, is the most commonly employed. Any move in the direction of the methodical and objective, any device that articulates shared assumptions, is likely to be positively helpful and is to be welcomed. The application of a linguistically motivated analysis to the text produced by the teacher new to interaction with a class is, I believe, potentially helpful enough to justify fully the expenditure of the time and resources required. Where tutor and student are familiar with such a model they have, for a start, a detailed set of meanings in common, a language in which the talk about the interaction in which one has participated and which the other has observed. Recorded and transcribed text need not be complete – need not even be very substantial, in order to provide evidence of readily identifiable mistakes that need not be repeated, and, as usefully, of identifiable successes – exchanges for example where pupils easily and correctly predicted what was to come, responded appropriately, and where the feedback move assured them of this appropriateness, and included usefully informative comment. This sort of detailed comment, that adheres closely to actually occurring text and emerges from analysis of it, seems to me to deserve the name of professional education. Within such a context criticism, and self-criticism, is acceptable. Students *do* make mistakes that characterise inexperience; they regularly, for example, underprepare those exchanges, the boundary exchanges, that have an organising function in relation to lessons. It is common to find framing moves, realised by a marker 'now' or 'well', but no clear focusing move, realised by a metastatement, that clearly announces the topic to pupils who have been obliged to turn attention, at the sound of a bell, from a totally different set of preoccupations. Students often are unaware of the passage of time, and in consequence fail to take up the option of a concluding boundary exchange, and lose the chance of communicating to those in the class the sense of intention fulfilled. Students do not always recognise the necessity, for those taught, of consistent, interpretable feedback. Need to reinitiate frequently is a pointer to mismatch between teachers' and pupils' assumptions at another level altogether than discourse. Brief analyses of this sort are more acceptable in general terms to students than are more general and global comments, and more important, they indicate the use of classroom strategies, couched in wholly non-technical terms and capable of virtually immediate implementation, that yet have a principled basis. The regular use of such analyses would be far from easy to organise or to implement. Considerable expenditure of time, and perhaps of other resources would be required, and would, I believe, be justified. The improvement of the experience of teaching practice, at just that sensitive and critical point where the efforts of the novice teacher are the subject of discussion with another who has the authority of experience, is important to everyone who shares concern for the quality of children's classroom experience.

Bibliography

Barnes, D., Britton, J. and Rosen, H. (1971, revised edn), *Language, the Learner and the School*, Harmondsworth, Penguin.

Barnes, D. and Todd, F. (1981), 'Talk in small learning groups: analysis of strategies', in Adelman, C. (ed.), *Uttering, Muttering*, London, Grant McIntyre.

Bateman, D. and Zidonis, F. (1966), *The Effect of a Study of Transformational Grammar on the Writings of 9th and 10th graders*, National Council for the Teaching of English, Research Report no. 6.

Bates, E. (1979), Review of S. Ervin-Tripp and C. Mitchell-Kernan, *Child Discourse, Language in Society*, vol. 8, no. 2, pp. 298-300.

Bellack, A.A., Kliebard, H.M., Hyman, R.I., and Smith, F.L. (1966), *The Language of the Classroom*, New York, Teachers' College Press.

Bereiter, C. and Engelmann, S. (1966), *Teaching Disadvantaged Children in the Pre-School*, New York, Prentice-Hall.

Berko-Gleason, J. and Weintraub, S. (1976), 'The acquisition of routines in child language – trick or treat', *Language in Society*, vol. 5, no. 2, pp. 126-37.

Bernstein, B. (1972), 'A critique of the concept of compensatory education', in Cazden, C.B., John, V.P., and Hymes, D. (eds), *Functions of Language in the Classroom*, New York, Teachers' College Press.

Berry, M. (1981), 'Polarity, ellipticity, elicitation and propositional development; their reference to the well formedness of an exchange: a discussion of Coulthard and Brazil's classes of move', *Nottingham Linguistic Circular*, vol. 10, no. 1.

Bloom, L. (1970), *Language Development: Form and Function in Emerging Grammars*, Cambridge, Mass., MIT Monograph no. 59.

Brown, R. (1974), *A First Language: The Early Stages*, London, Allen & Unwin.

Britton, J. (1970), *Language and Learning*, Harmondsworth, Penguin.

Bruner, J. (1974), 'The ontogenesis of speech acts', *Journal of Child Language*, vol. 2, no. 1, pp. 1-19.

Bullock, A. (1975), *A Language for Life: Report of a Committee of Enquiry under the Chairmanship of Sir Alan Bullock*, London, HMSO.

Burton, D. (1976), 'I think they know that – aspects of English work in primary classrooms', *Nottingham Linguistic Circular*, vol. 5, no. 1, pp. 22-35.

Burton, D. (1981), 'The sociolinguistic analysis of spoken discourse', in French, P., and Maclure, M. (eds), *Adult-Child Conversation*, London, Croom Helm.

Campbell, R. and Wales, R.J. (1970), 'The study of language acquisition', in Lyons, J. (ed.), *New Horizons in Linguistics*, Harmondsworth, Penguin.

Cazden, C.B. (1966), *Child Language and Education*, New York, Holt, Rinehart & Winston.

Cazden, C.B., John, V.P. and Hymes, D. (eds) (1972), *Functions of Language in the Classroom*, New York, Teachers' College Press.

Chanan, G. and Delamont, S. (eds) (1975), *Frontiers of Classroom Research*, Windsor, Berks., National Foundation for Educational Research.

Chomsky, N. (1957), *Syntactic Structures*, The Hague, Mouton.

Chomsky, N. (1959), Review of B.F. Skinner, *Verbal Behaviour*, *Language*, vol. 35, pp. 26-58.

Chomsky, N. (1965), *Aspects of the Theory of Syntax*, Cambridge, Mass., MIT Press.

Cohen, A.D. (1975), *A Sociolinguistic Approach to Bilingual Education*, Rowley, Mass., Newbury House.

Corsaro, W.A. (1977), 'The classification request as a feature of adult interaction styles with young children', *Language in Society*, vol. 6, no. 2, pp. 183-209.

Corsaro, W.A. (1979), 'We're friends right?' Children's use of access rituals in a nursery school, *Language in Society*, vol. 8, pp. 315-36.

Coulthard, R.M. (1969), 'A discussion of restricted and elaborated codes', *Educational Review*, vol. 22, no. 1, pp. 38-50.

Coulthard, R.M. (1975), 'Discourse analysis in English: a short review of the literature', *Linguistics and Language Teaching Abstraction*, vol. 8, no. 2, pp. 73-89.

Coulthard, R.M. and Brazil, D. (1979), *Exchange Structure*, Birmingham, University of Birmingham Discourse Monograph 5.

Cross, T.G. (1978), 'Mothers' speech and its association with the rate of linguistic development in young children', in Waterson, N. and Snow, C., *The Development of Communication*, London, John Wiley.

Derrick, J. (1966), *Teaching English to Immigrants*, London, Longman.

Derrick, J. (1977), *The Language Needs of Minority Group Children*, Windsor, Berks., National Foundation for Educational Research.

Ellis, R. and Wells, C.G. (1980), 'Enabling factors in adult-child discourse', *First Language*, vol. 1, pp. 46-62.

Ervin-Tripp, S. (1973), *Language Acquisition and Communicative Choice: Essays by Susan Ervin-Tripp*, ed Anwar S. Dil, Stanford, California, Stanford University Press.

Flanders, N.A. (1970), *Analysing Teaching Behaviour*, New York, Addison-Wesley.

Freeman, N. *et al.* (1979), 'Collaborative action rules in young children's understanding of locative instructions', unpublished presentation at Conference on Social Psychology and Language, University of Bristol, July.

French, P. and Maclure, M. (1981), *Adult-Child Conversation*, London, Croom Helm.

Gage, N.L. (ed.) (1963), *Handbook of Research on Teaching*, Chicago, Rand McNally.

Gahagan, D. and Gahagan, G. (1972), *Talk Reform*, London, Routledge & Kegan Paul.

Halliday, M.A.K. (1961), 'Categories of the theory of grammar', *Word*, vol. 17, pp. 241-92.

Halliday, M.A.K. (1969), 'Relevant models of language', *Educational Review*, vol. 23, no. 1, pp. 26-38.

Halliday, M.A.K. (1973), *Explorations in the Functions of Language*, London, Edward Arnold.

Halliday, M.A.K. (1975), *Learning How to Mean*, London, Edward Arnold.

Halliday, M.A.K. (1978), 'The significance of Bernstein's work for socio-linguistic theory', item no. 5 in *Language as Social Semiotic: the Social Interpretation of Language and Meaning*, London, Edward Arnold.

Hannam, C., Smyth, P. and Stephenson, N. (1976), *The First Year of Teaching*, Harmondsworth, Penguin.

Hasan, R. (1971), 'Syntax and semantics' in Morton, J. (ed.), *Biological and Social Factors on Psycholinguistics*, London, Logos Press.

Hill, D. (1976), *Teaching in Multi Racial Schools: a Guidebook*, London, Methuen.

Holbrook, D. (1961), *English for Maturity*, Cambridge, Cambridge University Press.

Holbrook, D. (1964), *English for the Rejected*, Cambridge, Cambridge University Press.

Holbrook, D. (1967), *The Exploring World: Creative Disciplines in the Education of English Teachers*, Cambridge, Cambridge University Press.

Horner, V.M. and Gussow, J.D. (1972), ' "John and Mary": a pilot study in linguistic ecology', in Cazden, C.B., John, V.P. and Hymes, D. (eds), *Functions of Language in the Classroom*, New York, Teachers' College Press.

Hunt, K. (1970), 'How little sentences grow into big ones', in Lester, M. (ed.), *Readings in Applied Transformational Grammar*, New York, Holt, Rinehart & Winston.

Huxley, R. and Ingram, E. (eds) (1971), *Language Acquisition: Models and Methods*, New York, Academic Press.

Hymes, D. (1972a), 'Models of the interaction of language and social life', in Gumperz, J.J. and Hymes, D. (eds), *Directions in Sociolinguistics: the Ethnography of Communication*, New York, Holt, Rinehart & Winston.

Hymes, D. (1972b), 'On communicative competence', in Pride, J. and Holmes, J. (eds), *Sociolinguistics*, Harmondsworth, Penguin.

Hymes, D. (1972c), 'Introduction', in Cazden, C.B., John, V.P. and
Hymes, D., *Functions of Language in the Classroom*, New York,
Teachers' College Press, Columbia University.

Jacobs, E. (1977), Review of Cicourel, A. *et al.*, *Language Use and
School Performance, Language in Society*, vol. 6, no. 2, pp. 288-93.

Jones, A. and Mulford, J. (eds) (1971), *Children Using Language: an
Approach to English in the Primary School*, London, Oxford
University Press.

Kaye, K. and Charney, R. (1974), 'Conversational A-symmetry between
mothers and children', *Journal of Child Language*, vol. 8, no. 1,
pp. 35-51.

Keenan, E.O. (1974), 'Conversational competence in children', *Journal
of Child Language*, vol. 1, no. 1, pp. 163-85.

Kochman, T. (1972), 'Black American speech events and a language
programme for the classroom' in Cazden, C.B., John, V.P. and
Hymes, D. (eds), *Functions of Language in the Classroom*, New
York, Teachers' College Press, Columbia University.

Labov, W. (1969), 'The logic of non-standard English', reprinted in
Giglioli, P. (ed.) (1972), *Language and Social Context*,
Harmondsworth, Penguin.

Lakoff, G. and Johnson, M. (1980), *Metaphors We Live By*, Chicago,
University of Chicago Press.

Lenneberg, E. (ed.) (1966), *New Directions in the Study of Language*,
Cambridge, Mass., MIT Press.

Luria, A.R. and Yudovich, F.I. (1968), *Speech and the Development
of Mental Processes in the Child*, ed J. Simon, London, Staples
Press.

McNeal, J. and Rogers, M. (eds) (1971), *The Multi Racial School*,
Harmondsworth, Penguin.

Martin, N. (1971), ' "What are they up to?" a study of a week's output
from three classes', in Jones, A. and Mulford, J. (eds), *Children
Using Language: An Approach to English in the Primary School*,
London, Oxford University Press.

Medley, D.M. and Mitzel, H.E. (1963), 'Measuring classroom behaviour
by systematic observation', in Gage, N.L. (ed.), *Handbook of
Research on Teaching*, Chicago, Rand McNally.

Mischler, E.G. (1972), 'Implications of teacher strategies for language
and cognition: observations in first grade classrooms', in Cazden,
C.B., John, V.P. and Hymes, D., *Functions of Language in the
Classroom*, Columbia, Teachers' College Press, pp. 267-99.

Opie, I. and Opie, P. (1967), *Lore and Language of Schoolchildren*,
Oxford, Oxford University Press.

Philips, S. (1972), 'Participant structures and communicative
competence: Warm Springs children in community and classroom',
in Cazden, C.B., John, V.P. and Hymes, D., *Functions of Language
in the Classroom*, Columbia, Teachers' College Press.

Reeder, K.F. (1975), 'Pre-school children's comprehension of
illocutionary force: an experimental psycholinguistic study',
unpublished doctoral thesis, University of Birmingham.

Reeder, K.F. (1980), 'The emergence of illocutionary skills', *Journal of Child Language*, vol. 7, pp. 13-28.

Rondal, J.A. (1980), 'Fathers' and mothers' speech in early language development', *Journal of Child Language*, vol. 7, pp. 353-69.

Rosen, H. (1972), *Language and Class: a Critical Look at the Theories of Basil Bernstein*, London, Falling Wall Press.

Rosen, H. and Burgess, T. (1980), *Languages and Dialects of London School Children: an Investigation*, London, Ward Lock Educational.

Rosen, C. and Rosen, H. (1973), *The Language of Primary School Children*, Harmondsworth, Penguin, for the Schools Council.

Rosenshine, B. and Furst, N. (1973), 'The use of direct observation to study teaching', in Travers, R.M.W. (ed.), *Second Handbook of Research on Teaching*, Chicago, Rand McNally.

Schiach, G.M. (1972), *Teach them to Speak*, London, Ward Lock.

Scope I: An Introductory Course for Immigrant Children, Stage I, (1969), London, Longman, for Books for Schools.

Scope 2: A Language Development Course for Second Stage Learners, (1972), London, Longman, for Books for Schools.

Shields, M.M. and Steiner, E. (1973), 'The language of 3-5 year olds in pre-school education', *Educational Research*, vol. 15, pp. 97-166.

Sinclair, J. McH. and Coulthard, R.M. (1975), *Towards an Analysis of Discourse: the English used by Teachers and Pupils*, London, Oxford University Press.

Simon, A. and Boyer, E.G. (eds) (1973), *Mirrors for Behaviour: An Anthology of Observation*, Philadelphia, Philadelphia University Press.

Skinner, B.F. (1957), *Verbal Behaviour*, New York, Appleton-Century-Crofts.

Snow, C. (1972), 'Mothers' speech to children learning language', *Child Development*, vol. 43, pp. 549-55.

Snow, C. (1977), 'The development of conversation between mothers and babies', *Journal of Child Language*, vol. 4, no. 1, pp. 1-22.

Snow, C. and Ferguson, C. (eds) (1977), *Talking to Children: Language Input and Acquisition*, Cambridge, Cambridge University Press.

Spolsky, B. and Cooper, R. (eds) (1977), *Frontiers of Bilingual Education*, Rowley, Mass., Newbury House.

Stern, H.H. (1972), 'Introduction', in Swain, M. (ed.), *Bilingual Schooling: Some Experiences in Canada and the United States*, Ontario Institute for Studies in Education.

Stubbs, M. (1976), *Language, Schools, and Classrooms*, London, Methuen.

Stubbs, M. (1980), *Language and Literacy: the Sociolinguistics of Reading and Writing*, London, Routledge & Kegan Paul.

Stubbs, M. and Robinson, B. (1979), *Analysing Classroom Language*, Milton Keynes, Open University, Course PE 232, block 5, part 1.

Tough, J. (1973), *Focus on Meaning: a Study of Children's Use of Language*, London, Allen & Unwin.

Tough, J. (1977), *The Development of Meaning*, London, Allen & Unwin.

Travers, R.M.W. (ed.) (1973), *Second Handbook of Research on Teaching*, Chicago, Rand McNally.

Twitchin, J. and Demuth, C. (eds) (1981), *Case Studies in Multi-Cultural Education: View from the Classroom*, London, BBC.

Vorster, J. (1975), 'Mommy-linguist: the case for Motherese', *Language*, vol. 37, pp. 281-313.

Waterson, N. and Snow, C. (1978), *The Development of Communication*, New York, John Wiley & Sons.

Weinreich, U. (1974), *Languages in Contact: Findings and Problems*, The Hague, Mouton.

Wells, C.G. (1975), 'Learning to code experience through language', *Journal of Child Language*, vol. 1, no. 2, pp. 243-71.

Wells, C.G. (1977), 'Language use and educational success: a response to Joan Tough's "The Development of Meaning" ', *Nottingham Linguistic Circular*, vol. 6, no. 2, pp. 52-71.

Wells, C.G. (1979), 'Influences of the home on language development', Bristol Working Papers in Language no. 1, University of Bristol, mimeo, pp. 29-51.

Wells, C.G. and Montgomery, M. (1981), 'Adult-child interaction at home and at school', in French, P. and Maclure, M., *Adult-Child Conversation*, London, Croom Helm.

Wight, J. *et al.* (1972), *Concept 7/9*, London, Edward Arnold, for the Schools Council.

Williams, F. (ed.) (1970), *Language and Poverty: Perspectives on a Theme*, Chicago, Markham.

Index